FOUNDA... ...
EDUCATION RESEARCH

M000214910

The theoretical components of research are some of the most complicated and challenging aspects for new researchers to understand. While relevant methodologies are routinely covered by textbooks, the theory behind the practice can remain unnecessarily opaque. In seven concise chapters *Foundations of Education Research* defines, discusses, and presents applications for the central components of research in order to provide researchers with a common ground from which to work. Including conceptual framework, epistemology, paradigm, theory, theoretical framework, and methodology/method, this book gives students the tools they need to understand existing education research literature and to produce theoretically grounded work of their own.

Beginning each chapter with perspectives from both novice and experienced researchers, this book is designed to help students achieve a deeper understanding of what is expected of them and ideas about how to achieve it. Guiding questions from both perspectives can assist researchers who are engaging with theory for the first time and those looking to improve their understanding of the fundamentals. Practice exercises and suggested reading lists at the end of each chapter offer students resources they can apply to their own research and thinking in concrete ways. A perfect accompaniment to standard research courses, this primer demystifies the jargon of education research in practical terms.

Joy Egbert is Professor of Education at Washington State University, Pullman, USA.

Sherry Sanden is Assistant Professor of Early Childhood Literacy at Illinois State University, USA.

FOUNDATIONS OF
EDUCATION RESEARCH

UNDERSTANDING
THEORETICAL
COMPONENTS

JOY EGBERT
AND
SHERRY SANDEN

Routledge
Taylor & Francis Group

NEW YORK AND LONDON

First published 2014
by Routledge
711 Third Avenue, New York, NY 10017

and by Routledge
2 Park Square, Milton Park, Abingdon, Oxon OX14 4RN

Routledge is an imprint of the Taylor & Francis Group, an informa business

Library of Congress Cataloging in Publication Data
Egbert, Joy.
    Foundations of education research : understanding theoretical components /
    Joy Egbert, Sherry Sanden.
      pages cm.
    Includes bibliographical references and index.
    1. Education—Research. 2. Education—Research—Methodology. I. Title.
    LB1028.E268 2013
    370.72—dc23
    2013020483

ISBN: 978-0-415-71576-8 (hbk)
ISBN: 978-0-415-71579-9 (pbk)
ISBN: 978-1-315-88051-8 (ebk)

Typeset in Minion and Scala
by EvS Communication Networx, Inc.

For Jamie and David, still and always the loves of my life.

Joy

To DES, whose support makes it all happen.
And to JPH, BLH, and ZCH, for always.

Sherry

Contents

Foreword

In *Foundations of Education Research: Understanding Theoretical Components,* Joy Egbert and Sherry Sanden address central components of research in order to give both novice and experienced researchers common ground from which to learn and grow. In assuming the roles of experienced and more novice researchers, Egbert and Sanden offer a unique approach for making these concepts that all researchers use both clear and precise. Instead of creating hypothetical examples to make these terms come to life, they turn to their lived experiences and the insights gleaned from them. Their voices as researchers at different places in their careers add a touch of authenticity and honesty that contributes to this text's interest and credibility. Topics that too often remain dryly explained become attention-grabbing and thought-provoking.

Beyond the clear, precise, and interesting presentation of their ideas, the authors add features that further the usefulness of this text. For example, they do not leave an ability to apply these terms to chance. By referencing methodologists as well as practitioners, they allow readers to receive information about the topics under consideration alongside examples of their use. In addition, the pedagogical pieces that Egbert and Sanden add to each chapter direct readers' attention to central messages which support their grasp of important ideas.

Foundations of Education Research: Understanding Theoretical Components offers the research community a timely and important text. Its terms hold long-standing importance and warrant a text that allows them to be understood and applied with insight and confidence. Egbert and Sanden accomplish this by making this text user friendly (important for those novice researchers whom they target) without sacrificing a heady and scholarly presentation of complex concepts (important for experienced researchers). I know of no book that explicitly addresses these concepts in such an engaging and informative manner. I welcome its addition for the research community. *Foundations of Education Research: Understanding Theoretical Components* deserves a place in the research courses we teach and on our bookshelves.

Mary F. Roe

Professor, Arizona State University

Preface

There is a critical lack of consistency across research communities, perspectives, and paradigms about what reports on research should look like and contain. Although researchers seem to agree that certain components are essential, they do not often define those components so that readers and other researchers can identify their perceptions or do not include some of the components that would allow readers to comprehend in a holistic way the import of the study. This is not a book on how to do research or on specific research methodologies—there are already many fine texts that address these issues. Rather, it provides a brief overview of some of the basic jargon of research and the components that are important to the research process regardless of a particular perspective. It reaches across viewpoints to address the specific, generic ideas that all studies should include in order for readers not only to understand the research but to be able to make educated judgments about it. This text is an attempt to come to a common understanding of the jargon of research and the components that are important to the research process.

This book briefly defines, discusses, and provides applications of the central components of research in order to give both novice and experienced researchers common ground from which to work. The book includes seven concise chapters focusing on the following components: conceptual framework, epistemology, paradigm, theory, theoretical framework, and methodology/method. These components are addressed through a series of questions whose answers are essential to understanding. Each chapter begins with anecdotes from a novice and an experienced researcher that set the stage for the chapter content. The final chapter addresses common misconceptions about research and offers advice for all researchers.

This book is intended to accompany any/every research methods text. It could easily be used by both graduate and undergraduate researchers in courses including Introduction to Research, Foundations of Research, Principles of Research, Qualitative Research, Quantitative Research, Writing the Doctoral Dissertation/Master's Thesis, and advanced research courses and seminars. In addition, scholars conducting research might use this book as a reference.

Acknowledgment

The authors wish to thank the many people who helped bring this book to press. These include first and foremost Stan Wakefield, whose perseverance and belief in this project made all the difference. Thanks to Rebecca Novack and the team at Routledge/Taylor & Francis. Appreciation for Dr. Barbara Ward and Dr. Tom Salsbury, who agreed to use this text in class because we asked them to. Also to all of the students who participated in the classes where it was used and gave us suggestions—thank you for your honesty and effort. Finally, thanks to Dr. HyunGyung Lee, who painstakingly corrected our mistakes, and the fabulous doctoral students in T&L 570, who were happy to help this book come to print.

1

FOUNDATIONS OF RESEARCH: CONCEPTUAL FRAMEWORK

Experienced researcher:

> *It's often hard to understand differences between how we think about and approach life and how we do the same for research. Although the approaches certainly have commonalities and affect each other, the words and ideas we use to understand research are specific to the endeavor in general and to each field in which it's undertaken. If these approaches and the terms we use to talk about them are confusing for experienced researchers, they have to be even more so for novices.*

Novice researcher:

> *As new researchers, my fellow doctoral students and I were astonished to discover how much we had to learn. While often confident in our content knowledge, the research component frequently left us traversing unfamiliar and confusing territory. For example, the sheer number of terms used*

to describe research work was daunting. Happily we immediately began to acquire research knowledge from our instructors and their use of scholarship that allowed us to see research terms in action. The bad news was the inconsistency with which experts in the field often utilized research terms and practices. Just when we thought we had acquired some conceptual knowledge of a research term, it was used in a completely different way that threw cold water on the spark of our understanding. How could we as newbie researchers ever hope to build our own capabilities when experts with decades of experience failed to cohere on basic research concepts?

In this chapter, we address the following questions:

- What are the research components and why are they important?
- What is a conceptual framework and why does it matter?
- What does conceptual framework use look like?
- Where does conceptual framework fit into a model of research components?

REFLECT: Before you read the chapter, think about how you would answer the questions above with your current knowledge.

What Are the Research Components and Why Are They Important?

This book briefly defines, discusses, and provides applications of the central theoretical components of research and their applications in order to give both novice and experienced researchers common ground from which to work. As we said in the preface, there is a critical lack of consistency across research communities, perspectives, and paradigms about what reports on research should look like and contain. Although researchers seem to agree that certain components are essential, they do not often define those components so that readers and other researchers can identify their perceptions, or they do not include some of the components that would allow readers to comprehend in a holistic way the import of the study. This is not a book on how to do research or on specific research methodologies—there are already many fine texts that address these issues. Rather, it is an attempt to clear the air, to come to a common understanding of the jargon of research and the components that are important to the research process regardless of a particular perspective. It reaches across viewpoints to address the ideas that all studies should include in order for readers not only to understand the research but to be able to make educated judgments about it.

In doing the research for the college course this book is based on and the book itself, it became very evident that across disciplines and even within them, research terms are defined and used in very different ways. In some cases the terms are used differently in similar contexts and in other cases many of the terms are used to mean the same thing. Words like "conceptual framework," "epistemology," " theoretical framework," and even "method" have come to imply so many different (or no specific) ideas that it makes conducting and consuming research more difficult than it has to be. However, there are important differences among these research components, and making those differences explicit may help to clarify not only the research process but our own positions and influences as researchers.

The seven terms we address in this book (*conceptual framework, epistemology, paradigm, theory, theoretical framework, methodology, method*) appear to us to be the most in need of clarity. They are the essential ideas that ground every research study and can have an impact on not only the development of the study but also how the data are analyzed and the results interpreted. If we want our research to be clearly understood and evaluated, it is obvious that we need to understand these concepts. There are additional terms that every researcher should explore but that are not emphasized in this text; these include ontology, or "views of reality" (see Johnson, 2008, for a simple and thorough explanation), and analysis and interpretation (see Chiseri-Strater & Sunstein, 2006; Plano-Clark & Creswell, 2010, for overviews).

In this book we propose specific definitions and uses of each of the component terms and we have put forward our view of how to define and talk about these components based on how they are understood and used across varying research perspectives. While we acknowledge that some readers may have alternative views about how to define and discuss these components, our discussion demonstrates the need for research groups or sub-fields at least to have common understandings in order to move research forward more easily. It also underscores the need for these components to be presented and explored specifically within research reports that are to be shared. We have found that this common ground makes a huge difference in how we think and write.

What Is a Conceptual Framework and Why Does It Matter?

In order to demonstrate the need for common understanding, we will begin with the term "conceptual framework." An analogy can help explain this component: Look at the portrait painting in Figure 1.1; it contains elements such as a background, facial features, clothing, and even text on the subject's lips. Viewers do not see the material on which the painting has been created—it can be made of any of myriad different materials, be an infinite variety of colors, and even take on different shapes. However, its function remains the same—to support and set off the painting. Important to note is that the painting's canvas *is not* part of the painting itself, but a separate, essential entity that the picture must have in order for it to hold together and to provide a

Figure 1.1 Painting by high school student Jamie Jessup. Used with permission.

foundation for the rest of the painting's elements. A conceptual framework works in these same ways in research.

We consider a conceptual framework as an **overall worldview**. It is an individual perspective defined not only by values and perceptions (Northcutt & McCoy, 2004), but also by the sum of one's experiences, beliefs, and knowledge from every facet of life, including, for example, gender, religious, family, political, social, academic, and environmental arenas. This view does not change often or easily. Conceptual framework is often used interchangeably with the term "paradigm" in the popular press, but these terms represent very different concepts in research (see chapter 3 for a discussion of paradigm). One's worldview influences the clothes one wears, the food one eats, the places one travels, and the charities to which one contributes. It also influences all of the components of research, although its impact may be hard to discover. For example, if I were raised in a religious tradition in which Truth was a central concept, I might ask research questions based in an epistemology (discussed in chapter 2) that emphasizes finding a "Truth" rather than seeking smaller "truths." Similarly, if I had experience with many cultures around the world, I might conduct research that encompasses a more global outlook than otherwise. Furthermore, if I adopted a passion for environmental causes from my parents, I might use this as one focus of my research even if it is not my field per se. Decisions that researchers make can be (and in our view, should overtly be) explained in part by the researcher's conceptual framework. This is because, as Borgatti (1999) notes:

> ... no matter how little you think you know about a topic, and how unbiased you think you are, it is impossible for a human being not to have preconceived notions, even if they are of a very general nature. ... The framework tends to guide what you notice ... and what you don't notice. In other words, you don't even notice things that don't fit your framework! We can never completely get around this problem, but we can reduce the problem considerably by simply making our implicit framework explicit. Once it is explicit, we can deliberately consider other frameworks ... (para. 3)

However, unlike some of the other concepts in this text such as theory and method, the discussion of the researcher's conceptual framework can be unwelcome in research in general; notions of research as "objective" often preclude its mention. We believe, along with Allen (2005) and others, that the idea that researchers can "turn off" their selves and ignore their beliefs and perceptions when constructing and carrying out research is problematic. The good news is that although in some venues researchers are still discouraged from being explicit about their conceptual frameworks, the explicit discussion of the impacts of religion, gender, sexual orientation, political stance, and other parts of our conceptual frameworks are now more accepted, and, in some venues, required. This is due in part to the trend toward more participant-centered and "action" research, where it becomes crucial to understand both the researcher's stance and the participants' beliefs in order to understand the interpretation of often complex and "messy" results (Johnson, 2008).

What Does Conceptual Framework Use Look Like?

The term "conceptual framework" is sometimes used interchangeably (and we say incorrectly) with what we call the theoretical framework, as in these examples from fields related to education:

> Through our analysis of the data, we identified two meta-themes: a) challenges and b) facilitators accompanying the transition to adoptive parenthood. Grounded theory methodology was used to develop these themes into a *conceptual framework* describing the transition to adoptive parenthood. This framework posits that each parent negotiates a particular set of challenges and facilitators associated with their specific adoption experience. In future, this framework can become a tool to assist adoptive parents and practitioners to proactively identify and address potential challenges during the transition to parenthood. (McKay & Ross, 2010, p. 604, italics added)

> A case study was conducted to identify the factors affecting the adoption of Dimenxian, which was a new educational computer game designed to teach Algebra to middle school students. The diffusion of innovations theory was used as the *conceptual framework* of this study. (Kebritchi, 2010, p. 256)

In the first example above, the term "conceptual framework" is used to refer to a practical model that the researchers suggest can also be a tool. In the second example, the authors use the term to refer to what we view as a theoretical framework, described further in chapter 5. Obviously some clarity is needed for this term!

Although not quite yet common in the academic literature itself, research journal forums are free to bring in aspects of personal conceptual frameworks and their effects on students, the field, data collection, and so on. These discussions are held around the articles in top level journals, but not often *in* the articles. For example, online or forum-type discussions might be focused like the following:

> Do you agree with the characterization of the spiritual beliefs and professional values of the Evangelical teachers in this article? Do you share the authors' opinion that dialogue with evangelical teachers is difficult as they hold a value system that is at odds with the others in the profession? (From the *TESOL Quarterly* Online Forum, Values in Language Teaching Board, http://communities.tesol.org/default.asp?action=9&boardid=5&read=2735&fid=426)

> Which article(s) in this special issue do you feel particularly relates to your teaching or your experience? And why? What experiences of yours speak to the issues raised and discussed in the article? (Race and TESOL Board, http://communities.tesol.org/default.asp?action=10&boardid=5&fid=416)

In some areas of research, particularly in relatively newer areas such as cultural studies and in certain journals that publish qualitative studies, researchers are expected to make their conceptual frameworks and specific aspects of their life view explicit; these aspects are even subjects of study themselves. For example, Huisman (2008) examines

> the dynamics of reciprocity and positionality in research. Drawing from research conducted with Bosnian Muslim refugees, the author

outlines three tensions she experienced and addresses how these tensions were related to her shifting and sometimes contradictory positionalities as a woman, a researcher, a friend, a graduate student, and as a person who was straddled between two classes. This is followed by a discussion about the lessons learned and the way the experiences shaped her current collaborative, community-based research project with Somali refugees. (p. 372)

Allen (2005) implies that the conceptual framework is ever expanding and that even the research itself has an impact on one's life view:

Objectivist approaches to positionality emphasise the "background thinking" that social researchers carry into the field, unexamined, as occupants of social positions that are class, gender etc. based. It follows that this (class, gendered) background thinking unconsciously influences the process of knowledge production ... I argue that constant exposure to the "disciplinary gaze" of [policy] funders means that the positionality of [researchers] is also moulded during the course of the academic career. This means that the positionality of [researchers] is not simply established within the field nor carried into the field. Rather, the positionality of [researchers] develops over time of constant exposure to the "disciplinary gaze" of research funders and manifests itself in what Foucault refers to as "docility", i.e. research practices intuitively and uncritically oriented to satisfying the needs and demands of research funders. (p. 989)

In other words, research and research gatekeepers can change the conceptual frameworks of academics, much as other events can throughout life. In the same way, the life views (conceptual frameworks) of researchers and even the personality traits that accompany those views can have an impact on research that, if examined, can help explain the overall endeavor.

How Should a Conceptual Framework Be Applied in Research?

If the researcher is explicit about the components of research that we discuss in this text (epistemology, paradigm, and so on), then the conceptual framework is either implied in these components or may not need to be explicitly stated. However, we believe that where it is relevant and makes a difference, it should be stated, however briefly, in order to help the reader better understand the research undertaking. This idea does not apply only in qualitative research; experimental researchers also make choices (e.g., which theory to tap, which literature to ground their study in, which questions to ask) based on their personal identities, and understanding these positions helps the reader discern the greater research context. For example, Vaughan, Rogers, Singhal, and Swalehe (2000) conducted an interesting experiment in Tanzania

> to measure the effects of a long-running entertainment-education radio soap opera, Twende na Wakati (Let's Go with the Times), on knowledge, attitudes, and adoption of human immunodeficiency virus (HIV)/acquired immune deficiency syndrome (AIDS) prevention behaviors are presented. Multiple independent measures of effects and the experimental design of this study confer strong internal and external validity regarding the results of this investigation. (p. 81)

To assist readers in better understanding the context of this experiment, the researchers could include information about their contacts/interest in this African country, their personal understanding of why entertainment education, particularly the show under investigation, is important, why they made specific decisions out of the number possible, and how the outcomes of the analysis matched their personal expectations. Although the study can stand alone as published, this additional information provides a frame that gives readers a deeper understanding of the study's meaning.

Where Does Conceptual Framework Fit Into a Model of Research Components?

As another analogy, and one we use throughout the text, if we conceive of research as a tree growing up from the ground, our conceptual framework can be thought of as the earth that surrounds and sustains the tree and from which it takes life-sustenance (as in Figure 1.2). No part of the tree (all the research components) can live without the earth, but it is invisible to and expressed through each part of the tree. So, we can picture conceptual framework in this analogy like the tree, supporting the seed of a research idea.

Another way to think of conceptual framework is as a large circle with permeable boundaries through which life ideas and experiences flow, as in Figure 1.3.

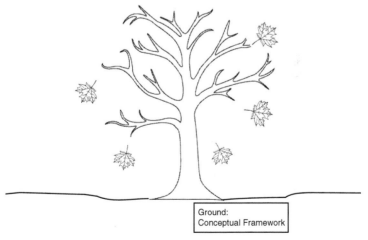

Ground:
Conceptual Framework

Figure 1.2 Tree diagram for conceptual framework

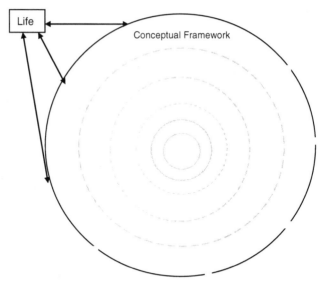

Figure 1.3 Circle diagram for conceptual framework

REFLECT: How do you picture your conceptual framework? Draw a picture of it here.

Conclusion

Research is not an objective endeavor, as much as we often try to have it look like one. The conceptual framework, or life view, of the researcher translates into each component of the research process in certain ways. Because researchers make decisions based on their own knowledge and experiences, research consumers are better served by having the subjectivity of the decision-making process made explicit through the components. The rest of this book focuses on defining and explaining the components and providing examples of how they work together to produce rigorous, clear, and meaningful research.

Guided Practice

1. Look at the articles in the appendix. Can you discern the authors' conceptual frameworks in any way? If so, how? What do they look like? How do they affect the decisions that the authors make about their research?
2. Write a short autobiography, outlining important ideas and events in your life and describing how these integrate to form your life view.

Further Reading

Milner, R. (2007). Race, culture, and researcher positionality: Working through dangers seen, unseen, and unforeseen. *Educational Researcher, 36*(7), 388–400.

Roberts, J. (2001). Dialogue, positionality and the legal framing of ethnographic research. *Sociological Research Online, 5*(4). Available at http://www.socresonline.org.uk/5/4/roberts.html

The role of the qualitative researcher: Positionality and reflexivity, ©2006–2010 British Educational Research Association. Available at http://www.bera.ac.uk/the-role-of-the-qualitative-researcher-positionality-and-reflexivity/

Widdowfield, R. (2000). The place of emotions in academic research. *Area, 32*(2), 199–208.

References

Allen, C. (2005). On the social relations of contract research production: Power, positionality, and epistemology in housing and urban research. *Housing Studies, 20*(6), 989–1007.

Borgatti, S. (1999). *Elements of Research*. Retrieved from http://www.analytictech.com/mb313/elements.htm

Chiseri-Strater, E., & Sunstein, B. (2006). *What works?: A practical guide for teacher research*. PortsmouH, NH: Heinemann.

Creswell, J. W. (2007). *Qualitative inquiry and research design: Choosing among five approaches* (2nd ed.). Thousand Oaks, CA: Sage.

Huisman, K. (2008). "Does this mean you're not going to come visit me anymore?": An inquiry into an ethics of reciprocity and positionality in feminist ethnographic research. *Sociological Inquiry, 7*(3), 372–396.

Johnson, A. (2008). *A short guide to action research*. Boston, MA: Allyn & Bacon/Pearson.

Kebritchi, M. (2010). Factors affecting teachers' adoption of educational computer games: A case study. *British Journal of Educational Technology, 41*(2), 256–270.

McKay, K., & Ross, L. (2010). The transition to adoptive parenthood: A pilot study of parents adopting in Ontario, Canada. *Children & Youth Services Review, 32*(4), 604–610.

Northcutt, N., & McCoy, D. (2004). *Interactive qualitative analysis: A systems method for qualitative research*. Thousand Oaks, CA: Sage.

Plano-Clark, V., & Creswell, J. (2010). *Understanding research: A consumer's guide*. Boston: Merrill/Pearson.

Vaughan, P., Rogers, E., Singhal, A., & Swahele, R. (2000). Entertainment education and HIV AIDS prevention: A field experiment in Tanzania. *Journal of Health Communication, 5*, 81–100.

2

INFLUENCES ON THE RESEARCH AND THE RESEARCHER: EPISTE-WHAT?

Novice Researcher:

> *Upon registering for my first semester of full-time doctoral studies, I saw a course titled "Education, Research, and Epistemology." As it was a required course in the college's research block, I dutifully signed up, even though "epistemology" was a word that I had never encountered. Seeking understanding from both a dictionary and Wikipedia were necessary before the semester started, since I didn't want to arrive the first day completely out of the loop. Even then, a reasonably understandable definition eluded me and I hoped that I would be able to catch on. All sources from which I sought information about this unfamiliar term included the phrase "theories of knowledge," which was not helpful. Knowledge was knowledge; why was it necessary to have theories about it? You either knew things or you didn't ... right? I had not occurred to me that the word "know" could or should be enclosed by quotation marks.*

Experienced Researcher:

> I've worked with a lot of new researchers over the years. They seem at first to flounder, to have no idea what questions to ask or what methods they should use or how they can/should look at their topic. I think in some ways they don't understand their own cognitive frameworks and how they translate into a research plan. Their research methods courses are often too short (with too much to cover) to help them figure out this transfer process. Students need to start with an awareness of how their views of the world (conceptual frameworks) shape their thinking and the individual epistemologies that arise out of this thinking. Exploring generic epistemologies like "feminism" or "social justice" is fine, but not everyone adheres to the same beliefs even within the same category, and new researchers need to be encouraged and supported to understand and explain their individual views of knowledge.

In this chapter, we address the following questions:

- How is epistemology defined?
- How is an epistemology formed, and can it change?
- What are some general epistemologies?
- How does epistemology relate to conceptual framework?
- How does epistemology support research?

REFLECT: Before you read this chapter, explain your understanding of the term "epistemology."

Episte-*what*?

In explaining the term "epistemology," the tendency in the literature seems to be to try to define the word in the vaguest terms possible. Creswell (2007) notes that across the literature the term "epistemology" has been equated with worldview, paradigm, ontology, and even methodology. One phrase, *theories of knowledge,* appears frequently. This is a definition for epistemology that is elegant and efficient, and yet is relatively ineffective in providing the fledging researcher with a comprehensive idea of the impact of epistemology on research. Another phrase, *ways of knowing*, is thrown around in discussions about epistemology and gets us closer to an understanding but still misses the mark. Because of the typically cryptic definitions assigned to the word *epistemology*, we start with what we hope is a more understandable way of describing the term because of our belief in the value of developing an agreed-upon set of labels and concepts to guide the research process. With common definitions, researchers can more easily focus on the content of research endeavors and engage more readily in conversations in the field. Therefore, we define epistemology as **the individual lens, created through our worldview, that we use to understand knowledge in the world**. This definition captures a number of elements that we will explore in order to provide a more substantial understanding of the impact of researchers' epistemologies on their research work.

To break this description down into its major parts, we begin with the idea of an **individual lens**. This part of the definition indicates that epistemology is unique for each individual and is used as a resource through which understanding takes place. Imagine putting on a pair of glasses, fitted just for you, that contain purple lenses. When you look around you, the world as you previously perceived it is different. While it contains the same mountains and trees and animals, they have all taken on a slightly distorted appearance. Nothing viewed through those purple lenses looks the same as it did before, and, of course, the view is different for the person standing next to you wearing glasses with green lenses. You are both looking at the same mountains and trees and animals, but the picture for that person is not the same as the one you are seeing. You each *know* something slightly different about the scene in front of you. So it is with an epistemology. The lenses that you "put on" and through which you see the world create for you your personal beliefs about knowledge.

Next we explore the idea that an epistemology is **created through our worldview**. As outlined in chapter 1, individuals possess unique conceptual frameworks, or combinations of beliefs and understandings based on the accumulation of experiences in which they have been immersed across their lifetime. Socioeconomic, cultural, and family backgrounds, learning encounters, professional experiences, personal interactions: The entire smorgasbord of circumstances and events that form a person's existence are responsible for creating for each individual a slightly different ability to perceive the world, including a unique understanding of knowledge. Hofer (2001) discusses the variety of approaches attempting to explain how our epistemological development occurs. Some models suggest that individuals progress through a series of stages in their understanding of knowledge, occurring simultaneously with their maturity, while an alternate approach explains that a system of beliefs about knowledge results more or less independently of individuals' aging or development. Another view explains the organization of individuals' epistemological beliefs as personal theories that may be specific to particular domains or contexts. Regardless, it is clear that the understandings and beliefs that we hold develop in conjunction with and because of our experiences.

Finally, we tackle the concept that an epistemology allows us to **understand knowledge in the world**. This is the place where the philosophical aspect of the definition rears its head, and where the definition begins to take on increasing significance for our research endeavors. On a broad level, understanding knowledge from an epistemological standpoint involves considering a number of questions, including what kinds of knowledge are possible and what the scope of knowledge is (Crotty, 2003). While the temptation for new researchers might be to avoid such abstract considerations and dive head-first into more "practical" research considerations, the danger with that approach lies in its inherent limiting of different ways of thinking (Paul & Marfo, 2001). Rather than having the ability to view knowledge through the purple or green or blue lenses, the researcher is stuck with only the yellow, eliminating all of the understandings that might have been possible if other options had been considered.

At a foundational level, to *know* something means **to believe it to be true**, although Shope (2002) acknowledges that even this basic definition has led to wide-ranging disagreements over the nuances of knowledge. To understand multiple views of knowledge it is important to consider how individuals acquire knowledge. For example, is everything we know a result of our experiences, or do we possess innate knowledge? How can we verify the reliability of those knowledge sources? It is also important to consider what we mean when we say we *know* something. If an individual *knows* something that someone else believes is erroneous, is it really knowledge? Do we know anything for sure?

It seems that a definition of *knowledge* raises more questions than it answers, but if we accept that our views of knowledge in general reflect our belief system about what is true, then we can begin to understand knowledge in terms of "truth" or "Truth." Note the purposeful use of the small "t" or the capital "T" here, because it indicates the way that the knowledge is viewed. Believing that something is Truth indicates an incontrovertible certainty of it, regardless of any individual's different understanding. In this view, a mountain is always the same mountain with the same properties, no matter who is viewing it, or even if no one is viewing it. It maintains an unbiased mountain-ness. On the other hand, a belief in a truth (or truths) acknowledges that particular certainties may vary and that no one individual's perspective provides the definitive understanding. A mountain viewed by one person may possess slightly different or completely different qualities than the mountain when viewed by someone else. From this perspective, the mountain-ness of it is dependent on who is looking at it.

Individuals possess theories about knowledge, whether or not they actively consider them, which results in their thinking in certain ways. Researchers cannot help but bring their beliefs about knowledge, their epistemology, to the forefront and put their understandings about knowledge to use in the ways they conduct their research. Considering the possibilities for beliefs about knowledge and then developing a personal system of beliefs allows researchers to put on their own unique epistemological lens through which to view their research topics.

What Are Some Epistemological Positions?

There exists a range of epistemological stances with an even larger array of possible combinations of beliefs about knowledge that individual researchers can hold. Each stance develops, as we have noted, based on an individual's experiences, and each stance results in research work that varies in its purpose and implementation. While the specific labels applied to differing epistemologies may vary, an explanation of some of the more agreed-upon classifications will aid in better understanding. Crotty (2003) identifies three general categories of epistemology, under which lie a variety of theoretical perspectives that guide research work.

Objectivism

An objectivist epistemology sustains the belief that meaning exists independent of the consciousness of any individual. An individual holding an objectivist epistemology will *know* that a mountain is a mountain is a mountain, no matter who looks at it. Within this belief system, there exists a Truth and it can be discovered if inquiry is performed in the right way. This has important implications for research because the researcher operating within an objectivist epistemology is in pursuit of an ultimate Truth. Research questions will ask about issues that prompt definitive answers, and the methodology will be designed to enable the researcher to state those answers based on evidentiary findings.

Holding an objectivist epistemological stance frequently leads researchers to adopt a theoretical perspective consistent with positivism or post-positivism. Crotty (2003) explains that a positivist perspective provides the opportunity to discover unbiased knowledge in which you hold the utmost confidence, regardless of context or circumstances, chiefly through a scientific method. A post-positivist perspective also privileges direct conclusions of fact resulting from scientific findings but calls into question researchers' absolute objectivity, thereby providing for some questioning over the possibility of researchers achieving absolute Truth.

Constructionism

Belief in a constructionist epistemology results in the rejection of the notion of objective Truth. Knowledge for each individual is viewed as a construction based on the individual's experiences. Since each person is likely to have experiences that vary from those of another, each individual's knowledge construction will differ. An individual operating within a constructionist epistemology will *know* that a mountain possesses certain characteristics, based on his or her experiences with it, just as another individual will *know* about the characteristics of the mountain based on his or her experiences. However, the knowledge held by the first person might not be the same knowledge held by the second because the experiences that caused each to know may have been different. Multiple truths exist, based on the experiences that have prompted knowledge construction for each individual.

One sub-category of constructionism is social constructionism, which acknowledges the impact of others around us and our social interactions with them, on our ways of discovering truths. Within this perspective, the construction of knowledge is viewed specifically as a result of our experiences with human practices that prompt understanding, which inherently vary from individual to individual.

Research conducted within a constructionist epistemology will allow experiences with objects of research to guide the understanding that is taken from the research. Questions will be asked that hope to reach one or more truths about the topic under exploration, with answers constructed from the array of events that occur during the study.

Subjectivism

Within a subjectivist epistemology an object contributes nothing to its meaning; understanding is wholly reliant on the meaning ascribed by the subject. Knowledge is based on an individual's perception of an object or event, regardless of the attributes of the object or event itself. Therefore, knowledge is considered to exist in a realm of uncertainty; nothing can exist as a permanent Truth because one's perceptions can change, altering what an individual knows. A subjectivist epistemology will result in differing understandings of the mountain by each individual that perceives it and none of the understandings is expected to achieve the label of Truth. One perspective operating within a subjectivist epistemology is post-modernism, which rejects any attempts to achieve a Truth or truth and instead relies on messages of ambiguity and discontinuity (Crotty, 2003) in attempts to achieve understanding.

Within subjectivism, multiple truths are expected and accepted in the development of knowledge. Research conducted within a subjectivist epistemology seeks to build an awareness of a concept by examining alternative perspectives of those people and artifacts that hold understanding about it and building some tentative truths from them.

How Does Epistemology Relate to Conceptual Framework?

We think of epistemology as a theoretical component of research arising from and part of one's conceptual framework. Our definition of epistemology acknowledges the impact of life experiences on the formation of the lenses through which researchers specifically understand knowledge. These life experiences form a conceptual framework, within which beliefs about knowledge develop. This development of an epistemology occurs within the broader context of the conceptual framework, which acts as a guide for the researcher's beliefs about truth and Truth.

REFLECT: Think about a belief you hold in your personal or professional life to which you would assign the label *Truth*. What background experiences have led you to that conclusion? Now answer the same questions for the label *truth*.

How Does Epistemology Support Research?

The way researchers regard knowledge, both its acquisition and it potential for establishing truth or Truth, will impact the research they conduct. The questions they ask, the methods they use to collect data, and the meaning they ascribe to their results are all dependent on the epistemological lens through which they view knowledge. For example, a researcher who works within an objectivist epistemology will seek definitive answers to topics of interest because he or she believes in the existence of an objective Truth, which can be discovered if an appropriate inquiry is conducted. Experimental methods might be utilized based on a perception of their ability to provide hard answers to research questions. On the other hand, researchers operating behind the lens of subjectivism do not assume that an objective Truth is somewhere out there waiting to be discovered, so they do not typically bother asking questions to which a simple explanation is obvious. Rather, an exploration may allow for greater understanding based on interpretations ascribed by the researchers themselves but it is not presumed that their viewpoint is the only one possible based on the results. Qualitative methods might be applied in order to privilege researcher and participant insights in reaching greater understanding of the research topic. It is possible, although uncommon, for researchers to work from different epistemological viewpoints depending on the topic and context of their research. Like conceptual framework, epistemology is not set in stone and can fluctuate.

Unfortunately too many researchers fail to make their epistemology explicit in the dissemination of their research work. However, a careful examination of the author's writing often allows the reader to decipher the researcher's position regarding the possibilities for the research to result in Truth. For example, the following is Lee's (2008) description of a research synthesis of studies exploring the effects of test-driven external accountability policies:

> ... this review of large-scale studies using national data can make a timely and important contribution to policy discussion by producing more generalizable knowledge on the effects of high-stakes testing policy on the basis of common national benchmarks for the comparison of student achievement outcomes. The meta-analysis of 76 effect-size estimates drawn from 14 selected studies showed a modestly positive policy effect on average but no significant effect on narrowing the racial achievement gap ... This article raises questions about the scientific basis of NCLB and state accountability policy and possible

social consequences of the policy on the basis of inconclusive evidence and/or false premises about the policy impact on student achievement. (pp. 628–629)

Lee gives the impression that the failure to demonstrate a significant impact on a statistical analysis of the data provides grounds to doubt the feasibility of the policy in question. While not stated explicitly, we are left with the notion that evidence provided by these results is capable of providing us with a Truth on which to base decision-making. This belief, founded in an objectivist epistemology, results in Lee's exploration of independent and dependent variables, analytical samples and methods, and statistical and practical significance in studies under consideration, to determine their fitness for the label of scientific research.

Contrast this with Bernal's (1998) candid explanation of the epistemology she utilizes in her work:

... a Chicana epistemology must be concerned with the knowledge about Chicanas—about who generates an understanding of their experiences, and how this knowledge is legitimized or not legitimized. It questions objectivity, a universal foundation of knowledge, and the Western dichotomies of mind versus body, subject versus object, objective truth versus subjective emotion, and male versus female. In this sense, a Chicana epistemology maintains connections to indigenous roots by embracing dualities that are necessary and complementary qualities, and by challenging dichotomies that offer opposition without reconciliation. (p. 4)

Bernal is very clear about her subjectivist belief that knowledge can be found in multiple arenas and is the direct result of the perceptions of one's experiences. Obviously, multiple truths can be garnered from attention to such standpoints. In Bernal's work, pursued through a subjectivist lens, knowledge is garnered from the words of research participants, who provide their own unique perspectives regarding their experiences.

It is important to note that we do not claim that any epistemology can be deemed "better" than another; studies from different perspectives all add to the body of knowledge in different and useful ways.

How Does Epistemology Fit Into the Developing Models?

The model we introduced in chapter 1 is presented again in Figure 2.1 with the addition of epistemology. The tree model shows epistemology rooted in and growing from the conceptual framework. The circle diagram (Figure 2.2) also shows how epistemology is embedded within the conceptual framework and is open to its influence.

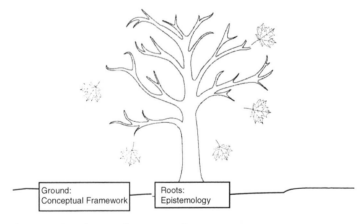

Figure 2.1 Tree diagram for epistemology

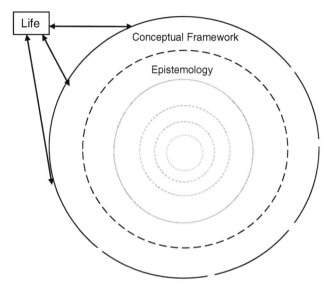

Figure 2.2 Circle diagram for epistemology

Conclusion

An essential beginning step for research endeavors is the consideration of the beliefs we hold regarding knowledge and its possibilities for aiding us in acquiring truth about our areas of interest. Holding in mind our view of where knowledge comes from and where it might lead us will provide guidance in the ways that we craft our research projects, from the questions we ask to the conclusions we draw. At this initial stage, our epistemological beliefs will lead us to consider the paradigms under which we can begin to pursue answers to our inquiry, a topic explored in the next chapter.

Guided Practice

1. Look at the studies included in the appendix. Scan each with an eye toward identifying the author's view of knowledge and consider the following questions: In which of the

broad epistemological categories do you see the researcher's work encased? Does the author view the knowledge he or she hopes to gain as a Truth or a truth or as multiple truths? What background experiences might have led the researcher to hold that view?

2. Choose a research topic of interest. Referring back to the conceptual framework that you began to form in the previous chapter, think about the background experiences that might impact how you view knowledge around this topic. Consider whether you believe that you can acquire a Truth or a truth or multiple truths about your topic of interest. How might your beliefs impact your research work?

Further Reading

Blaauw, M., & Pritchard, D. (2005). *Epistemology A-Z*. New York, NY: Palgrave Macmillan.

Objectivism 101: Tools for Living. (2006). Available at http://objectivism101.com/

Pallas, A. M. (2001). Preparing education doctoral students for epistemological diversity. *Educational Researcher, 30*(5), 6–11.

References

Bernal, D. D. (1998). Using a Chicana feminist epistemology in educational research. *Harvard Educational Review, 68*(4), 1–23.

Creswell, J. (2007). Qualitative inquiry and research design: Choosing among five approaches (2nd ed.). Thousand Oaks, CA: Sage.

Crotty, M. (2003). *The foundations of social research: Meaning and perspective in the research process*. London, England: Sage.

Hofer, B. K. (2001). Personal epistemology research: Implications for learning and teaching. *Journal of Educational Psychology Review, 13*(4), 353–383.

Lee, J. (2008). Is test-driven external accountability effective? Synthesizing the evidence from cross-state causal-comparative and correlational studies. *Review of Educational Research, 71*(3), 608–644.

Paul, J. L., & Marfo, K. (2001). Preparation of educational researchers in philosophical foundations of inquiry. *Review of Educational Research, 71*(4), 525–547.

Shope, R. K. (2002). Conditions and analyses of knowing. In P. K. Moser (Ed.), *The Oxford handbook of epistemology* (pp. 25–70). New York, NY: Oxford University Press.

3

RESEARCH PARADIGMS

Novice researcher:

By the time I was expected to use the word "paradigm" in relation to my doctoral work, I had a little more experience under my belt and was better able to relate these new research concepts to my course work. Besides, the word paradigm, unlike the unfamiliar term "epistemology," is actually recognizable to people outside academia. Of course, in the research world, concepts have a tendency to take on new and sometimes nuanced meanings, but at least the use of paradigms to explain one's perspective was not a completely unfamiliar idea. In fact, after studying the definitions of some of the more commonly described research paradigms, I became comfortable placing a label on my beliefs regarding teacher learning, my topic of study. My comfort level began to drop in only one class period, however, as I listened to my classmates proclaim the paradigms in which their studies would be situated, and no one was in my camp. When my turn to explain my position came around, I asked, rather hesitantly, "Is it okay if I'm a structuralist?"

Experienced researcher:

> Most students with whom I've worked initially understand the word "para-digm" as used in the popular press sense—of a "big idea" of some sort. In a way that understanding is valid, but conceptual frameworks and episte-mologies can also be seen as big ideas. Students need to know what the differences are among all of these big ideas. A second issue is that novice researchers can get caught up in a certain paradigmatic trend and feel pressure to follow it. Many of my graduate students have felt compelled to call themselves post-modernists when they have no idea of what a mod-ernist is and how to be "post" it. "Post-modernism" is another expression that, like paradigm, is freely used throughout both the popular and aca-demic presses, but which, upon closer investigation, turns out to be used in enough different ways as to make it almost meaningless. One of my colleagues recently cautioned me against a prescriptive use of research vo-cabulary, but, as a researcher working in the field of second language, I see it as a dire necessity in order to avoid confusion and mistaken identities.

In this chapter, we address the following questions:

- How is paradigm defined?
- What is the difference between conceptual framework, epistemology, and paradigm?
- What are some paradigms?
- What does paradigm use look like?
- How should a paradigm be applied in research?
- How does paradigm fit into the developing models?

REFLECT: Before you read the chapter, think about how you would answer the questions above with your current knowledge.

How Is Paradigm Defined?

The term "paradigm" is often used in the popular press (i.e., newspapers, magazines, Web sites) to mean a general idea about something; however, it is also used in enough different contexts to make it difficult to discern the underlying meaning of the word. For example, in an opinion piece on the widely read Time.com Web site, the author states that "the network is the key structure, or paradigm, or whatever you want to call it, of this century" (Grossman, 2008). In other words, the author defines paradigm as both a physical entity and a central idea, something like a "networkness" paradigm. In another article on the Time site, "stronger principles of accountability and transparency and integrity and sound practices" are seen as a new paradigm in banking (Mayer & Robinson, 2009). In this case paradigm is seen as a set of principles. In another instance, Jay Leno's first retirement from his long-running television talk show "Tonight" was noted as a paradigm change in late-night television. It seems that paradigm in this example indicates personnel!

The term "paradigm" is used in as many diverse ways in the academic literature as in the popular press. Some look at it as a researcher's overall conceptual framework (discussed in chapter 1), such as "My paradigm is liberal/environmental/social justice." In other cases, it is used in the same way as the popular press to mean a new idea or application. For example, Dunlap and Van Liere (2008) use it to indicate a way of looking at a field in general, Murawski and Hughes (2009) as a new application of information, and linguists as a pattern or model. Authors such as Kuhn (1962), who popularized the term "paradigm" in relation to scientific inquiry, equate paradigm to theoretical orientation in research. Others apply the term to what we call in chapter 6 the methodological framework of a study (e.g., qualitative or quantitative). A more generic definition is that a paradigm is "A set of assumptions, concepts, values, and practices that constitutes a way of viewing reality for the community that shares them, especially in an intellectual discipline" (Answers.com, n.d.).

While technically the term can be defined in any of these ways, it is not profitable to use it so broadly in the research literature—it cannot mean everything to everyone, or it ends up meaning nothing clear to anyone. Therefore, after studying the ways that paradigms are actually used in the literature, we understand a paradigm to be **a researcher's *specific stance* on how knowledge** (as defined by that same researcher's epistemological perspective about the nature of knowledge) **can be revealed**. As discussed in the next chapter, our paradigm supports the theories and methodological frameworks that we choose.

What makes a paradigm a paradigm? Chalmers (1982, p. 91) provides a useful general guideline, pointing out that a paradigm has five observable components:

1. Explicitly stated laws and theoretical assumptions.
2. Standard ways of applying the fundamental laws to a variety of situations.
3. Instrumentation and instrumental techniques that bring the laws of the paradigm to bear on the real world.
4. General metaphysical principles that guide work within the paradigm.
5. General methodological prescriptions about how to conduct work within the paradigm.

Understanding and acknowledging our research paradigm is focal because "within the research process the beliefs a researcher holds will reflect in the way the research is designed, how data is both collected and analyzed and how research results are presented. For the researcher it is important to recognize their paradigm, it allows them to identify their role in the research process, determine the course of any research project and distinguish other perspectives" (Belbase, 2007, n.p.). In addition, the explicit mention of the researcher's paradigm allows the consumers of the research to better assess it.

What's the Difference Between Conceptual Framework, Epistemology, and Paradigm?

In strictly a research sense, we separate paradigm from conceptual framework and epistemology by thinking of it as a narrower and more explicit position than the latter two. Our paradigm, like the rest of our perceptions, is influenced by our conceptual framework (worldview) and epistemology (whether we believe there is Truth or truths). Paradigms are how we think that Truth (or truths) can be *uncovered* (if they can). In this way, paradigm is a more specific statement of our general epistemology.

What Are Some Paradigms?

Some of the perspectives that comprise paradigms were mentioned as arising from certain epistemologies in chapter 2. Across academic fields there are four general categories of paradigms that are commonly recognized in the literature. These are structuralist, interpretivist, critical, and constructivist. Each category contains a number of specific paradigms, and each paradigm is associated with its own theories and methodological frameworks, discussed later in this text. Although the definitions of at least some of the categories are contested in the academic literature, a basic overview will facilitate additional reading.

Positivist

Researchers holding this view believe that knowledge is based on observed experience (this is part of their epistemology) and can be obtained through experiment. In this perspective, knowledge (Truth) is objective, measurable, and generalizable. Positivism underscores the systematic "scientific method" that emphasizes logic and empirical results and works toward the verification of hypotheses. Peters' (1999) explanation of structuralism/poststructuralism in education is a good place to start additional reading on this category. This category encompasses structuralism and its outgrowths such as functionalism.

Interpretivist (Post-Positivist)

A reaction to positivism, interpretivist paradigms in general hold that objectivity is a useful but not necessarily attainable ideal, particularly in natural settings such as classrooms. The "post-" paradigms underscore that reality is multilayered and complex and a single event can have multiple interpretations (coming from a constructivist or subjectivist epistemology). Researchers using an interpretivist paradigm emphasize human interaction with phenomena in their daily lives and suggest a mix of qualitative and quantitative methodological frameworks. An excellent overview of this category can be found at Ryder's *Contemporary Philosophy, Critical Theory and Postmodern Thought* Web site, which includes, among others, poststructuralist and post-modern paradigms.

Critical

Although some scholars believe that a critical paradigm is a natural extension of the interpretivist, others underscore the different foci of these categories. Criticality emphasizes oppression and the lived experiences of people in the contexts in which they live and work, grounded in a subjectivist epistemology. Scholars in this category point out that truths can be revealed by exploring the existing political conditions and contradictions and the hidden agendas and benefits of the current social order. They stress the importance of building awareness of multiple realities and allowing diverse voices to come to the fore. Researchers holding gender/feminist (see, for example, Switala, 1999), race (Parker & Lynn, 2002), sexual orientation/identity (Watson, 2005), and other epistemologies that focus on social justice often use this lens to guide their research decisions.

Constructivist

Although some scholars include this paradigm in the interpretivist category, as it becomes more well-developed it has taken on more of its own category. Constructivism emphasizes that reality is viewed and interpreted by the individual and group—it is not objective and cannot be measured through experiment. In other words, knowledge is subjective, contextualized, and personally experienced rather than acquired from or imposed from outside, and language and prior knowledge mediate individual realities and therefore must be explored. From a constructivist view, findings "are *literally created* as the investigation proceeds" through interaction between the researcher and the people and objects being researched (Guba & Lincoln, 1998, p. 111, italics in original).

Flexibility of Paradigms

All of these categories and the specific paradigms within them have been subject to both strong support and vehement criticism in the literature. Kim (2003) provides a useful resource from the field of organizational learning that outlines some of these arguments. It would be a mistake, however, to think of these categories as discrete, immutable entities. In fact, as each of the paradigms continues to develop and to migrate to additional academic fields, the criteria for establishing a single paradigm becomes more obscured. Schofield-Clark (n.d.), for example, describes how the critical and constructivist paradigms might usefully overlap, and Schultz and Hatch (1996) argue that multi-paradigm approaches can yield fruitful results. It is important to note that assuming or assigning a specific paradigmatic label is not the goal of understanding paradigms; rather, the objective is the recognition by both the researcher(s) and the consumers of the research of the researcher's stance in order to be able to better understand and evaluate research studies.

Reflect: Some authors identify these as paradigms, others as epistemologies or theories. Look up their definitions on the Web. What do you think?

- Existentialism
- Pragmatism
- Post-foundationalism
- Post-colonialism
- New-ageism

What Does Paradigm Use Look Like?

Although researchers do not usually make their paradigms explicit by applying a label, readers can understand from the features of the study where the researcher's work is grounded. For example, if the researcher is using an experimental methodology, we can assume that he comes from a positivist paradigm for this study, or if the researcher is using an existing body of literature to fit her study into, we can understand that this researcher might be taking an interpretivist stance.

Take, for example, the abstract from Egbert, Paulus, and Nakamichi (2002):

This purpose of this study is to examine how language teachers apply practical experiences from computer-assisted language learning (CALL) coursework to their teaching. It also examines ways in which teachers continue their CALL professional development. Participants in the study were 20 English as a second language and foreign language teachers who had, within the last 4 years, completed the same graduate-level CALL course and who are currently teaching. Surveys and follow-up interviews explored how participants learn about CALL activities; how what they learned in the course interacts with their current teaching contexts; the factors that influence whether or not they use technology in their classrooms; and how they continue to acquire and master new ideas in CALL. The findings support previous research on technology teacher education as it suggests that teachers who use CALL activities are often those teachers who had experience with CALL prior to taking the course; that lack of time, support, and resources prohibits the use of CALL activities in some classrooms; and that colleagues are the most common resource of new CALL activity ideas outside of formal coursework. Implications for teacher education are that teachers learn better in situated contexts, and technology courses should be designed accordingly. (p. 108)

First, the focus on the experiences of the teachers, rather than an experimental treatment, gives us a clue that the authors' paradigm in this study is not positivistic—or at least not strictly so. In addition, the fact that the authors tie the study closely to previous research suggests a specific paradigmatic view. Finally, that a specific focus on politics/social justice/advocacy has not been included shows that the authors are probably not using a critical stance. Clearly, this study has come from an interpretivist/constructivist view.

Now contrast the Egbert et al. (2002) study with this description from Nuthmann, Engbert, and Kliegl (2007):

Fixation durations in reading are longer for within-word fixation positions close to word center than for positions near word boundaries. This counterintuitive result was termed the Inverted-Optimal Viewing Position (IOVP) effect. We proposed an explanation of the effect based on error-correction of mislocated fixations [Nuthmann, A., Engbert, R., & Kliegl, R. (2005)]. Mislocated fixations during reading and the inverted optimal viewing position effect [*Vision Research, 45,* 2201–2217], that suggests that the IOVP effect is not related to word processing. Here we demonstrate the existence of an IOVP effect in "mindless reading", a z-string scanning task. We compare the results from experimental data with results obtained from computer simulations of a simple model of the IOVP effect and discuss alternative accounts. We conclude that oculomotor errors, which often induce mislocalized fixations, represent the most important source of the IOVP effect.(p. 990)

Notice that the authors "proposed an explanation." In other words, they asserted a hypothesis. In addition, the authors rely on experimental data and come to one certain conclusion. Clearly, these authors are working from a positivist stance.

How Should a Paradigm Be Applied in Research?

We advocate making a paradigm explicit so that the researcher and the reader have a basis for their interaction during the study description. In a section on researcher positionality (or positionalities, per Srivastava, 2006) that is becoming more commonly found in qualitative research reports, researchers can briefly explain their epistemological grounding and the paradigmatic foundation of the study. They can then explore in the discussion how this, or other paradigms, might affect the results of the study. (For an interesting argument on the benefits and disadvantages of expressing positionality in research, see Allies, 1999.)

For example, one student researcher explained the genesis of her epistemology and where she believed she fit paradigmatically in this way:

Through my professional career, I have observed innumerable examples of what I believe is true about the fraternity/sorority experience for most undergraduate students; Greek affiliation adds value and contributes to leadership development for college students. I also recognize that there are examples of negative Greek experiences for students, although I believe the benefits typically outweigh the negative aspects of fraternity and sorority membership. This study of the lives and leader identity development process for Greek students will provide a unique view into a student culture often misunderstood, vilified in the media, and questioned (negatively) in the literature. Through this study, I will be able to assert my particular finding as true rather than True, thus making my paradigm post-structural. Because I believe there is value added to the collegiate experience through fraternity/sorority affiliation, I believe my findings will show positive contributions in the areas I am studying, and these will be true, at least to a certain degree, for other campuses and college students as well. Others conducting a similar study may find a different truth, as campus and regional culture will influence individuals; nonetheless, I believe there will be similarities in the two truths.

Such a statement can reveal the biases that all researchers have. It can also provide information that clarifies for the reader and assists the reader in evaluating the study's conclusions.

In another example of expressing positionality, McLaughlin (2001) explains:

The researcher is of Papua New Guinea origin. Being a product of the PNG education system, and presently a resident of Australia, she is able to bring to the research understanding, insight, and passion found mainly in "insider" research. A critical issue which relates to insider researcher is the need for constant reflexivity, critical thinking in the research processes, the researcher's relationships and the quality and richness of data and analysis. In this study, the experiences of the researcher position her to empathise with the research participants. The ability to empathise created a relationship of trust through which location of the recipients in PNG became possible. (p. 10)

McLaughlin also explains her post-colonial/critical paradigm to very clearly frame her research. Because she set up the context of this study so visibly, the decisions she made about theory, questions, and research methods in the study make sense to the reader.

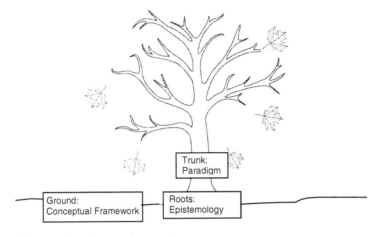

Figure 3.1 Tree diagram for paradigm

How Does Paradigm Fit Into the Developing Models?

The models we introduced in chapter 1 and grew in chapter 2 are presented again with the addition of paradigm. The tree model (Figure 3.1) shows the research paradigm (the tree trunk) arising from the epistemology (the roots), which is grounded in the researcher's overall conceptual framework (ground). The circle diagram (Figure 3.2) shows how each of the components is open to the influence of the others.

Conclusion

Novice and experienced researchers alike need to reflect on their paradigms in order to produce research that is consistent within itself and comprehendible to its consumers. Research from every paradigm, and from overlaps among them, adds to our overall understandings and provides multiple perspectives that, in turn, inform our use of paradigms in research. Perhaps more important, our paradigms support our use of theory, described in the next chapter.

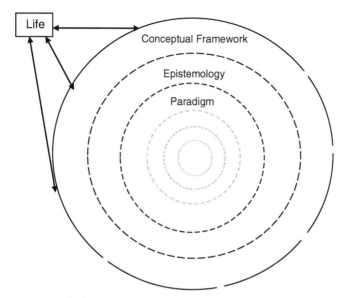

Figure 3.2 Circle diagram for paradigm

Guided Practice

1. The following are statements that novice researchers have made about their paradigms for a specific research study that they intended to conduct. From which paradigm do you think they see themselves coming? How do you see their paradigms?
   - I think that the impact of teacher quality on student achievement is undeniable. This fits with my epistemology because my background as a teacher and as a teacher educator has led to my unshakable belief in high-quality professional development to positively impact student literacy success.
   - I will examine how systems—even liberating and transgressive ones—play a part in limiting and even silencing voices with such things as policies and practices.

- I will explore how literature may affect change when students are engaged with it. However, I'm not sure what (if any) those changes are or how great those changes will be. Additionally, I believe that if changes do occur, they can and will be different for each individual reader.
- I will try to investigate whether there are stress and anxiety factors that affect EFL (English as a Foreign Language) students' learning of new literacies.
- Because children's realistic fiction books reflect real-life situations similar to EFL learners' own lives, my research will explore how, with careful consideration of the needs of learners at different levels and ages, creative curriculum design, and implementation, children's realistic fiction books can facilitate Taiwanese EFL learners' learning effectively.
- I believe the extensive reading that I will examine is only one effective way to facilitate EFL acquisition and its content needs to be adjusted to the sociocultural context it is situated in.

2. Review the articles in the appendix for indications of the authors' paradigms. What do you find?

Further Reading

Onwuegbuzie, A. J. (2002). Positivists, post-positivists, post-structuralists, and post-modernists: Why can't we all get along? Towards a framework for unifying research paradigms. *Education, 122*(3), 518–530.

Onwuegbuzie, A., & Leech. N. (2005). Taking the "Q" out of research: Teaching research methodology courses without the divide between quantitative and qualitative paradigms. *Quality and Quantity, 39*, 267–296.

References

Allies, L. (1999, September). *Positionality in life history research.* Paper presented at the British Educational Research Association Annual Conference, University of Sussex at Brighton. Retrieved from http://www.leeds.ac.uk/educol/documents/00001204.htm

Answers.com. (n.d.). http://www.answers.com/topic/paradigm

Belbase, S. (2007). *Research paradigms: Politics of researchers.* Retrieved from http://www.tesionline.com/intl/indepth.jsp?id=1124

Chalmers, A. (1982). *What is this thing called science?* Queensland, Australia: University of Queensland.

Dunlap, R., & Van Liere, K. (2008). The "new environmental paradigm." *Journal of Environmental Education, 40*(1), 19–28.

Egbert, J., Paulus, T., & Nakamichi, Y. (2002). The impact of CALL instruction on classroom computer use: A foundation for rethinking technology in teacher education. *Language Learning & Technology, 6*(3), 108–126.

Grossman, L. (2008, August 18). *Now in paper-vision: Does it matter that McCain is a NOOb?* Retrieved November 26, 2009, from http://techland.com/2008/08/18/now_in_papervision_does_it_mat/

Guba, E., & Lincoln, Y. (1998). Competing paradigms in qualitative research. In N. Denzin & Y. Lincoln (Eds.), *Handbook of qualitative research* (pp. 105–117). Thousand Oaks, CA: Sage.

Kim, S. (2003). Research paradigms in organizational learning and performance: Competing modes of inquiry. *Information Technology, Learning, and Performance Journal, 21*(1), 9–18.

Kuhn, T. (1962). *The structure of scientific revolutions.* Chicago, IL: University of Chicago Press.

Mayer, C., & Robinson, S. (2009, May 25). Gordon Brown: "Sometimes a crisis forces change." Retrieved November 26, 2009, from http://www.time.com/time/world/article/0,8599,1887600,00.html

McLaughlin, J. (2001, December). *Accommodating perceptions, searching for authenticity and decolonising methodology: The case of the Australia/Papua New Guinea secondary school students' project.* Paper presented at the 29th ANZCIES Conference, Curtin University of Technology, Perth. Retrieved from http://eprints.qut.edu.au/7574/

Murawski, W., & Hughes, C. (2009). Response to intervention, collaboration, and co-teaching: A logical combination for successful systemic change. *Preventing School Failure, 53*(4), 267–77.

Nuthmann, A., Engbert, R., & Kliegl, E. (2007). The IOVP effect in mindless reading: Experiment and modeling. *Vision Research, 47*(7), 990–1002.

Parker, L., & Lynn, M. (2002). What's race got to do with it? Critical race theory's conflicts with and connections to qualitative research methodology and epistemology. *Qualitative Inquiry, 8*(1), 7–22.

Peters, M. (1999). Poststructuralism and education. Retrieved from http://www.

ffst.hr/ENCYCLOPAEDIA/doku.php?id=poststructuralism_and_philosophy_of_education

Ryder, M. (n.d.). *Contemporary philosophy, critical theory and postmodern thought.* Retrieved from http://carbon.ucdenver.edu/~mryder/itc_data/postmodern.html

Schofield-Clark, L. (n.d.). Critical theory and constructivism: Theory and methods for the teens and the new media @ home project. Retrieved December 13, 2009, from http://www.colorado.edu/Journalism/mcm/qmr-crit-theory.htm

Schultz. M., & Hatch, M. (1996). Living with multiple paradigms: The case of paradigm interplay in organizational culture studies. *The Academy of Management Review, 2*(2), 529–557.

Srivastava, P. (2006). Reconciling multiple researcher positionalities and languages in international research. *Research in Comparative and International Education, 1*(3). Retrieved from http://www.wwwords.co.uk/pdf/freetoview.asp?j=rcie&vol=1&issue=3&year=2006&article=2_Srivastava_RCIE_1_3_web

Switala, K. (1999). Feminist theory website. Retrieved from http://www.cddc.vt.edu/feminism/enin.html

Watson, K. (2005). Queer theory. *Group Analysis, 38*(1), 67–81.

4

RESEARCH AND THEORY:
JUST A HUNCH OR SOMETHING MORE?

Novice Researcher:

> *A course in our doctoral program was designed to aid us in learning to form theoretical frameworks on which to base our research work. We read numerous studies to gain a better understanding of how researchers outlined their research base, and we learned to recognize the ways that authors wrote up their findings so that readers could pick out the theories around which the work was formed. It all seemed to make sense and allowed those of us who had been wondering how to organize our ideas to breathe a sigh of relief. All was well until the day on which we were expected to begin to form theoretical frameworks that related to our own research work. Many of us came to the same conclusion: What had seemed a magical formulation by the published authors was actually the accumulation and integration of knowledge about theories that we didn't possess. We had great ideas about our topics and we had done some reading to learn about*

the great ideas of others. Were those great ideas, both our own and those of others, enough to assign the label "theory"? When did a great idea take that immense leap into the realm of theory?

Experienced Researcher:

When working with novice researchers I've noticed that they have two main concerns with theory—first, many of them believe that they must use a theory verbatim in their research and are worried when it doesn't suffice. The second is that they are not sure what theory really is if it's not designated with a capital "T" in its title (e.g., the Theory of Relativity or Game Theory). Understanding these two issues would go a long way toward helping researchers frame their early studies clearly and consistently.

In this chapter, we address the following questions:

- How is theory defined for research purposes?
- What is the connection between paradigm and theory?
- How does theory support research work?
- How does theory fit within the developing models?

REFLECT: Before you read the chapter, think about how you would answer the questions above with your current knowledge.

How Is Theory Defined?

As is common with many research terms, the word "theory" is viewed differently when considered within the context of research endeavors than when it is used in everyday discourse. Wikipedia (2010) states that "in everyday language a theory means a hunch or speculation" (para. 1), while its scientific definition carries a much more stringent requirement. When used in the empirical realm, the purpose of a theory is to explain a set of circumstances with a reliable degree of accuracy. In an everyday encounter, we would have no qualms about expressing our personal theory that the cloud configurations seen on a given day will most likely lead to rain, as few of our listeners will hold us accountable if the clouds suddenly clear and the sun emerges. Unless we are meteorology school graduates, our theory about the weather is viewed as simply a guess based on our past experiences. In this case, the weather theory we so nonchalantly utter is not held to any sort of scientific certainty.

All bets are off, on the other hand, if that same theory is the basis for a weather report published under the guise of meteorological science. When theory is viewed within the context of a scientific or research endeavor, it is held to a much higher standard. A certain level of accuracy is assumed, and evidence for the claim must be made empirically. In other words, in a research context the term "theory" goes beyond a mere guess or hunch. We define theory, for the purposes of research, as **a reasonable, systematic, investigable, modifiable explanation of certain facts or phenomena that may help to predict an outcome**.

This definition raises the bar above household use regarding the ability of a theory to be a reliable explanation for a phenomenon under consideration. First, the requirement that a theory be **reasonable** emphasizes the need for the explanation to make sense. As Anfara and Mertz (2006) assert, once we understand a theory, it should seem obvious to the point that it prompts us to wonder at the fact that no one has thought of it before to explain the phenomenon in question. Kerlinger (1986) emphasizes that a theory must be **systematic**, outlining relationships between principles of the phenomenon. A useful theory must be **investigable** and **modifiable**, allowing room for exploration and growth with the advent of new discoveries. McMillan and Schumacher (2001) point out that a theory should always be considered a tentative explanation and should allow room for further investigation and revision. Finally, perhaps the most important attribute of a theory lies in its ability to go beyond a mere explanation to providing the means to **predict an outcome.** As Eisner (1993) states, "The adequacy of such explanations is tested not only by their appeal, their cogency, and their aesthetic quality, but by the extent to which they can be used to help us anticipate, if not control, the future" (p. vii).

While our definition describes the characteristics required to move a good guess into the realm of a research theory, the way theories are regarded is dependent on the field in which they are being created and used. For example, Bogdan and Biklen (2002) explain that while theory in quantitative research is sometimes restricted to "a systematically stated and testable set of propositions" (p. 22), the term "theory" in qualitative research provides "a way of looking at the world" (p. 22). They emphasize that regardless of the orientation used to view theory, it provides a means for allowing research accounts to build upon one another instead of existing in isolation.

Scholars (Alexander, 1987; Langenbach, Vaughn, & Aagaard, 1994) have pointed out that there are far fewer theories in the natural sciences than in the social sciences and that modifying theories is a much more cataclysmic event in the natural sciences (Anfara & Mertz, 2006). For an explanation of this trend we can rely on our understanding of epistemology and paradigm and the ways that they influence research endeavors. For example, research in the natural sciences tends to be more reliant on empirical work viewed from an objectivist perspective; findings can demonstrate a Truth that achieves a level of general agreement by most in the field. Until that Truth is shown to be faulty, the theory holds. Theories in this area include the Big Bang Theory (see, for example, Netting, 2013), the Theory of Evolution (Darwin, 1859/2011), and the Laws of Gravitation (Johnson, 2013). Research in the social sciences, on the other hand, is often conducted outside an objectivist epistemology, where multiple perspectives might be used to view a phenomenon. Findings may lead to numerous truths which result in a temporary theory that may be subsequently challenged by views through other perspectives. Therefore, a theory in social sciences tends to be more fluid in explaining phenomena in question and may meet the characteristics of a theory in different ways. Among many current theories used in the social sciences are some developed decades ago, including Constructivist Theory (Bruner, 1990, 1996), Situated Learning Theory (Lave & Wenger, 1990), and the Theory of Reasoned Action (Fishbein & Ajzen, 1975).

Connecting Paradigm and Theory

We defined a paradigm as the way that a researcher feels that knowledge can be revealed, based on his or her epistemology, or the belief in the existence of Truth or truths. Researchers' paradigms impact their use of theory based on whether or not they feel the theory can contribute to the understanding of their area of inquiry. Researchers holding a positivist paradigm, for example, may look for theoretical support within empirical findings, while researchers working from a critical paradigm may seek out theories resulting from the multiple truths of social justice research. A researcher's paradigm will guide his or her pursuit of the knowledge that can be gained through theories.

REFLECT: Try to name some claims or explanations of phenomena, in your own field or outside it, that might be labeled *theory*. Do they meet the criteria named above that allow the term *theory* to be applied?

How Does Theory Support Research Work?

In developing a research agenda, a researcher often relies on a number of things to formulate a plan for inquiry, including past experiences, observable needs, and curiosity regarding a particular situation. In addition, an exploration of others' theories on a topic often promotes additional impetus for inquiry, along with providing a framework on which an examination could ensue. Reading scholarship that has been written by others can provide information about what has already been established and what remains to be uncovered. It allows a researcher to see the lens through which the phenomenon in question has been viewed by others and perhaps consider an alternate perspective that would reveal additional information. This discussion/ analysis is typically included in research studies as a literature review.

Dressman and McCarthey (2004) propose some additional ways that the use of theory can support research endeavors. They state that the use of existing theories to ground a research study may prompt it to become bigger than just the localized context in which it is conducted, allowing findings from the new study to morph into and expand the broader research agenda. In addition, they suggest that previously proposed theories provide an outside basis of comparison, perhaps prompting realization of ways that current findings are consistent with existing scholarship or ways that they contradict past conclusions. For example, a researcher might include in the implications section of a study a discussion of how the theory used in the analysis could be employed profitably to examine a related concept.

Of course, the challenge lies in finding a theory that will be useful for a particular topic of inquiry. In order to allow theory to support research work, it is necessary to find past scholarship that provides relevant background information for the topic and that contains a sufficient base for forming a new line of investigation. A reasonable line must be able to be drawn between prior findings and the new area of inquiry. In one research example, Eun (2008) proposes the use of Vygotsky's sociocultural theory to better understand teacher professional development. Throughout the work he explains how elements of Vygotsky's theory connect to teachers' needs for professional learning. Eun acknowledges that Vygotsky's developmental theory was mainly concerned with children but demonstrates how those same theoretical concepts can be applied to adult learning as well. He notes the importance of using theory to support his inquiry, stating that "grounding professional development in a theoretical framework is not only important in revealing the process of development itself but also for devising plans that contribute to the effectiveness of professional development programs" (p. 135). Eun's ability to draw connections between an established theory and his own research endeavors demonstrates the usefulness of the theory to support his area or field of interest.

An area of concern for new researchers is how to locate theories that will prove useful in their own research activities. Experienced researchers make this part of the process look easy in their prolific use of established scholarship to ground their work. However, to the neophyte researcher, the number of possible theories and combinations of theories that exists is daunting. How can you find just the right theory that will meet the usefulness criteria that will allow your own research to prosper? How can you know that there isn't some better choice out there somewhere, if only you were better informed? Researchers who have been working in the field for a while might remind their protégés that at one time they too did not hold that accumulated knowledge; it became second nature only after years of reading and working in the field. While there might exist in each discipline manuals that list and explain theories considered relevant, only an ongoing effort to gain knowledge through examination of existing scholarship will allow that theoretical knowledge to become a part of a researcher's professional repertoire.

A further area of confusion for neophyte researchers is whether a "theory" is less worthy of respect and subsequent use in research work than a "Theory." Must research be based on a Theory with an official title, one that is universally recognized, or are the theories proposed in everyday scholarship sufficient foundation for ongoing studies? The Eun (2008) study discussed earlier relies on a connection with Vygotsky's sociocultural theory of development. Kearney and Hyle (2003) base their study of loss experienced as a result of organizational change on the Kübler-Ross (1969) model of the stages of grief. Both of these theories are well-known in their fields and lend an air of credibility to their use in research studies. However, the fact that a theory does not hold an immediately recognizable label does not preclude it from being a valuable foundation for ongoing research.

A useful example can be seen in Kirkland and Jackson's (2009) ethnographic study of the literacy practices viewed through symbolic patterns used by young black males to shape their coolness. These researchers consolidated theories defining literacy as multiple sign and symbol systems that reflect sociocultural practices, citing a number of authors from whom they draw support:

> In this article, we define literacy broadly, as a cultural practice that is embedded in social and cultural phenomena, such as coolness (Dyson, 2003; Freire & Macedo, 1987; Gee, 2001; Mahiri, 2004). Literacy, then, is capable of operating from a diversity of representational systems, particularly when combining written and oral forms with visual, gestural, and other kinds of symbols. This definition of literacy is consistent with scholars who see literacy as a cultural practice that involves multiple sign-and-symbol systems (Hull & Nelson, 2005; New London Group, 1996). That is, individuals and groups communicate by using more than just words (Bean & Harper, 2008; Gallego & Hollingsworth, 2000; New London Group, 1996). (p. 279)

Kirkland and Jackson do not feel the need to apply the grand title of Theory to every idea that they cite in framing their research work, although the propositions they put forth might certainly be considered theories. An explanation for a phenomenon does not require the label "Theory" to be useful to research work. To be useful, a theory (which, by being a theory, meets the expectations outlined in the first section of this chapter) needs to meet the criterion of relevancy, meaning that a reasonable relationship can be inferred between past scholarship and the present curiosity that is leading the way to new research work.

How Does Theory Fit Into the Developing Models?

The models continue to grow with the addition of the research term "theory." On the tree model, the outgrowth of theories from the paradigm indicates the possibility of different branches of research work to be informed by multiple theories stemming from a supporting paradigm (see Figure 4.1). Again, the circle diagram shows how each of the components is open to the influence of the others, with the circles becoming smaller as the research becomes more specific (see Figure 4.2).

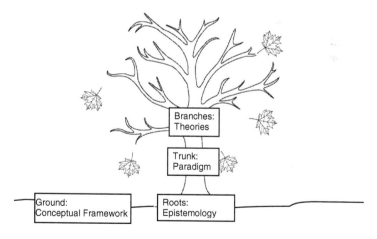

Figure 4.1 Tree diagram for theories

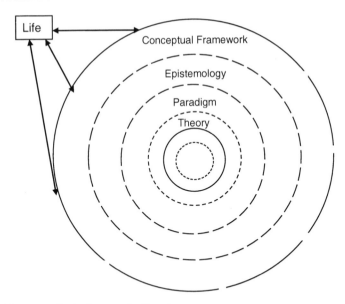

Figure 4.2 Circle diagram for theories

Conclusion

The use of theories to ground our research inquiries provides numerous benefits, not the least of which is the ability to connect beyond our local context. Plugging into the wisdom of the larger field allows us to see what has come before and to envision what may be on the horizon. It provides a background against which our own research endeavors can be measured and within with our findings can be viewed. New and experienced researchers alike benefit from a foundation on which to build ongoing research efforts, secure in the knowledge that their own endeavors aid in building theory for the future of the field.

Guided Practice

1. Examine the research studies in the appendix, watching for ways that the authors use one or more theories to ground their own work. Are the theories ones you recognize or are they less well-known explanations? What impact do the theories appear to have on the research studies being conducted?

2. Reflecting on your epistemology and your paradigm that you have begun to develop over the last two chapters, consider them in the context of a research interest you hold. Locate some research articles that discuss your topic, paying attention to the theories that authors of the articles use in their literature reviews. Are any of the theories consistent with your own perspectives on the topic?

Further Reading

For links to a number of notable theories in a variety of areas: http://en.wikipedia.org/wiki/Theory

Learning-Theories.com: http://www.learning-theories.com/

Theory into Practice Database: http://tip.psychology.org/

References

Alexander, J. C. (1987). The centrality of the classics. In A. Giddens & J. Turner (Eds.), *Social theory today* (pp. 11–57). Stanford, CA: Stanford University Press.

Anfara, V. A., & Mertz, N. T. (2006). Introduction. In V. A. Anfara & N. T. Mertz (Eds.), *Theoretical frameworks in qualitative research* (pp. xiii–xxxii). Thousand Oaks, CA: Sage.

Bogdan, R. C., & Biklen, S. K. (2002). Qualitative research for education: An introduction to theory and methods (4th ed.). Boston, MA: Allyn & Bacon.

Botelho, M. J., & Rudman, M. K. (2009). *Critical multicultural analysis of children's literature: Mirrors, windows, and doors.* New York, NY: Routledge.

Bruner, J. (1990). *Acts of meaning.* Cambridge, MA: Harvard University Press.

Bruner, J. (1996). *The culture of education,* Cambridge, MA: Harvard University Press.

Darwin, C. (1859/2011). *On the origin of species*. Greensboro, NC: Empire Books.

Dressman, M., & McCarthey, S. J. (2004). Epistemology, methodology, and theories. In N. K. Duke & M. H. Mallete (Eds.), *Literacy research methodologies* (pp. 322–346). New York, NY: Guilford.

Eisner, E. W. (1993). Foreword. In D. J. Flinders & G. E. Mills (Eds.), *Theory and concepts in qualitative research: Perceptions from the field* (pp. vii–ix). New York, NY: Teachers College Press.

Eun, B. (2008). Making connections: Grounding professional development in the developmental theories of Vygotsky. *The Teacher Educator, 43*, 134–155.

Fishbein, M., & Ajzen, I. (1975). *Belief, attitude, intention, and behavior: An introduction to theory and research*. Reading, MA: Addison-Wesley.

Johnson, W. (2013). Newton's laws of motion and gravitation. *e-how*. Retrieved from http://www.ehow.com/about_6330995_newton_s-laws-motion-_amp_-gravitation.html

Kearney, K. S., & Hyle, A. E. (2003). The grief cycle and educational change: The Kubler-Ross contribution. *Planning and Change, 34*(1, 2), 32–57.

Kerlinger, F. N. (1986). *Foundations of behavioral research* (3rd ed.). New York, NY: Holt, Rinehart, & Winston.

Kirkland, D. E., & Jackson, A. (2009). "We real cool": Toward a theory of black masculine literacies. *Reading Research Quarterly, 44*(3), 278–297.

Kübler-Ross, E. (1969). *On death and dying*. New York, NY: Routledge.

Langenbach, M., Vaughn, C., & Aagaard, L. (1994). *An introduction to educational research*. Boston, MA: Allyn & Bacon.

Lave, J., & Wenger, E. (1990). *Situated learning: Legitimate peripheral participation*. Cambridge, England: Cambridge University Press.

McMillan, J. H., & Schumacher, S. (2001). *Research in education: A conceptual introduction* (5th ed.). New York, NY: Longman.

Netting, R. (2013). The Big Bang. NASA Science/Astrophysics. Retrieved from http://science.nasa.gov/astrophysics/focus-areas/what-powered-the-big-bang/

Wikipedia. (2010, January 19). Theory. Retrieved January 27, 2010, from http://en.wikipedia.org/w/index.php?title=Theory&oldid=338768275

5

THEORETICAL FRAMEWORKS: YOU CAN'T HAVE A HOW WITHOUT A WHY

Experienced Researcher:

One of the most important components in any research study is the theoretical framework, and it's the one that makes or breaks an article in any paradigm. Although some researchers using a grounded qualitative methodology suggest that researchers should approach their data with a blank slate, the futility of trying to take the humanness out of research makes this approach problematic. A theoretical framework is not only necessary from a theoretical standpoint but it also helps novice researchers clearly plan and conduct their studies. While it may also focus the researcher to the extent that some important findings may be missed, peer review and other research processes can help to mitigate this issue.

Novice Researcher:

> I think the theoretical framework is a double-edged sword. On the one hand, I can use established theories consistent with my research interests to set up a framework on which to build a study. As a newbie still uncertain about the feasibility of my own inquiry, this kind of structure, grounded in past scholarship, is reassuring. On the other hand, knowing the significance of a theoretical framework to the quality of a research study creates a lot of pressure. My newness to the field causes me to question my ability to assemble a reasonable framework that supports my study. What if my inexperience means that I lack sufficient background in theories to be able to form a reasonable theoretical framework? What if there are some powerful theories out there that I'm just not aware of? And once I've found some theories that meet the needs of my study, how can I know that I've consolidated them to best support its outcome?

In this chapter, we address the following questions:

- What is a theoretical framework?
- Why is it important?
- How do researchers identify/find/create a theoretical framework?
- How do researchers use one?
- How does theoretical framework fit into the model?

REFLECT: Before you read the chapter, think about how you would answer the questions above with your current knowledge.

On Monina Escalada's *Writing the Thesis Outline: Theoretical Framework* blog page (2009; and elsewhere in her research-focused site), hundreds of students writing research proposals have left comments like these:

- My thesis title is on poverty alleviation ... what theories are best suited in my topic? i'll use this in my theoretical framework ... help me plssss.... thank you!!!
- Hello everyone, can someone help here plzzzzzzzzzzzzzz. i dnt know how to write theoretical framework. can someone give me ideas ... here is the research: The main aim of the research is to explore the possibilities of pro-poor tourism development and its contribution towards poverty alleviation, social and environmental conservation
- Hi! I have trouble with my theoretical part as well. My topic is education related "Immigrant children in Greek classes and fulfillment of their educational rights". I thought of referring to what Cummins, Banks etc. have to say about the topic and then to what are the educational rights of children in general but I don't think this will qualify as the theoretical part! Any instructions as to how to form it?

While some novice researchers know what a theoretical framework is in at least a general way, others do not really know, or they believe that it is only a complete theory that a famous scholar has developed (usually with a capital "T" as discussed in the previous chapter, i.e., Big Bang Theory, the Theory of Relativity, or Critical Theory). To understand theoretical frameworks better, Escalada's advice to most of the questions she receives is the same as that we suggested in chapter 4—read. For researchers to understand the term as used in their field and to be able to construct a theoretical framework that is relevant to their research, they must be familiar with the theories in their field that can be gained through a review of the literature (this issue is discussed further later in this chapter).

An established theory can certainly be used verbatim as a theoretical framework for a study if it is relevant (as described in the previous chapter), but often the questions in which a researcher is interested make it necessary to look beyond the limits of a single theory to blend elements from a number of theories. In its broadest sense, then, a theoretical framework can be defined as an **integration of the theoretical concepts that apply to the problem under investigation**.

Fortunately for Escalada's students and other novice researchers, the term "theoretical framework" has fairly common agreement across fields and types of research. This is not to say that everyone adheres to this common definition and its use, but rather that many good examples and explanations exist. Here are definitions from a variety of resources:

> why or how we expect certain relationships to exist and the nature and direction of the relationships among the variables of interest. A schematic diagram [or model of the] theoretical framework will also help the reader to visualize the theorized relationships. (blurtit, n.d.)

> [T]he theoretical framework is supposed to help the reader make logical sense of the relationships of the variables and factors that have been deemed relevant/important to the problem. It provides [definition of the] relationships between all the variables so the reader can understand the theorized relationships between them. Or, a theoretical framework is a collection of interrelated concepts, like a theory but not necessarily so well worked-out. A theoretical framework guides your research, determining what things you will measure, and what statistical relationships you will look for. (wiki.answers, n.d.)

Although Anfara and Mertz (2006) claim that the term "theoretical framework" is not well defined for qualitative research, their definition is in keeping with many of the others we found while reviewing the literature for this chapter. In their in-depth text on theoretical frameworks in qualitative research, the authors define theoretical framework as "any empirical or quasi-empirical theory of social and/or psychological processes, at a variety of levels (grand, mid-range, explanatory), that can be applied to the understanding of phenomena" (p. xxvii).

Another simple explanation that agrees with the others is provided by Zeidler (n.d.), who suggests that a theoretical framework can be "viewed as the answer to two basic questions:

1. What is the problem?
2. Why is your approach a feasible solution?" (n.p.)

Why Is It Important?

Here again, most resources agree on why it is important to have (and we would add to *clearly state*) a study's theoretical framework. Cline (n.d.) explains:

1. Since the problem is a function of its framework, *the problem can be better articulated and understood* if its basic system is well understood and articulated. Additional facets of the problem may be generated as a result, and the known facets will take on greater clarity and form.
2. When the framework is well articulated, it is possible *to conceive and consider alternative frameworks*. The explication of behaviorist theory in early psychology made it possible to see what its strengths and weaknesses were and to develop alternative theories that ultimately had high payoff (e.g., the advent of cognitive psychology and one of its offspring, Rational Emotive Therapy). Given several possible frameworks, the researcher chooses from among them on the basis of criteria such as heuristic value, inclusiveness, efficiency, and the like. The power of a proposed solution to the problem may thus be considerably enhanced.
3. The explication of a theoretical framework or logical structure provides focus to all the subsequent steps in planning and carrying out the proposed inquiry, e.g., charting variables and their relationships. It makes it possible to generate a relatively complex set of objectives and questions; it provides a basis for including and excluding literature and

research that is actually related to the inquiry by identifying the variables of greatest interest and concern; and it provides focus to the inquirer's procedural planning and choices from initial design selection, through instrument development or adoption, to the organization, analysis and interpretation of data, e.g., research design, statistical tests, making sense of empirical findings.

4. Perhaps most important is the impact of the explicit theoretical structure on subsequent inquiry in the same area. The investigation no longer hangs loose but becomes part of a line or tradition of inquiry which other researchers can check, replicate or build upon. Knowledge growth in a field becomes an additive phenomenon of increasingly useful structures or concepts with which inquirers can work.

5. Without a clear explication of the problem and a workable perspective with which to view it, it is likely that the research project will be flawed by uncontrolled extraneous variables, overlooked variables, faulty instruments, haphazard procedures and the like.

Herek (1995) agrees with Cline's points, noting that the theoretical framework strengthens the researcher's research in several ways:

- First, explicitly stating of the theoretical assumptions permits them to be evaluated critically.
- Second, the theoretical framework connects the researcher to existing knowledge.
- Third, articulating the theoretical assumptions of a research project forces the investigator to address questions of why and how. It permits researchers to move from simply describing a phenomenon observed to generalizing about various aspects of that phenomenon to other groups and situations.
- Finally, having a theory helps to identify the limits to those generalizations. (p. 86)

In other words, the theoretical framework provides the "why" of the study. Clearly, the use of a theoretical framework can have a major impact not only on how the study is conducted but the ways in which it is received and interpreted by its readers.

How Do Researchers Identify/Find/Create a Theoretical Framework?

As noted previously, reading literature in the area of interest is mandatory for developing a theoretical framework. Review of the literature can help researchers uncover the frameworks being used in their and other fields and explore how they are used. Researchers may find that a previous study uses a framework that is directly relevant to the current problem being addressed and fits with their notions of Truth/truth, and so use the same framework. Alternatively, the framework used in one or more studies could suggest a general set of important concepts but encourage the researcher to continue to look for additional theoretical concepts that are more specific to the questions at hand. On her Web site, Escalada (2009) provides these steps for novice researchers to create a theoretical framework:

1. Examine your thesis title or topic and research problem.
2. Brainstorm on what you consider to be the key variables in your research. Read and review related literature to find answers to your research question.
3. List the constructs and variables that might be relevant to your study.
4. Review the social science theories (communication, psychology, sociology, anthropology) and choose the theory that can best explain the relationships between the key variables in your study.
5. Discuss the assumptions or propositions of this theory and point out their relevance to your research.

We would add that the researcher cannot only choose a theory but a number of theories or even elements of theories. In addition, researchers should not be afraid to look outside their own bounded field for theoretical elements that might apply; interesting new perspectives on phenomena often arise in exactly this way.

Another example of a process of choosing and using a theoretical framework is shown in Figure 5.1, in which a researcher follows a thought process similar to the steps proposed by Escalada (2009). The figure demonstrates the direct relationship of the theoretical framework to formulation of the research questions and the methods used to answer them.

How Do Researchers Use a Theoretical Framework?

In Figure 5.1 the theoretical framework grounds the planning of the study. In this hypothetical study, the framework is used to

Guiding Question	Example/Answer
What's your topic?	My topic is student engagement in literacy in technology-enhanced classrooms.
What is it that you wonder?	I wonder what engages English as a Second Language (ESL) students in reading.
Why do you wonder this?	Because reading in a second language is different from reading in a first language, and ESL learners are often disengaged in reading. Since it's important to their lives, it's important for teachers to understand it deeply.
What specifically do you want to find out?	If technology use helps engage students in reading.
Why is this important?	Because engagement is one important component that leads to achievement, and technology use seems to be engaging. There might be some overlap between reading and technology use.

Figure 5.1 Process for developing a theoretical framework

Guiding Question	Example/Answer
What are the main components of your question that you need to find out about?	Engagement, reading, and technology.
What IS engagement?	Well, it's evidenced by students spending more time on task and having greater focus and a positive attitude.
Why do you think technology use MIGHT engage students?	Because when used effectively it's more fun than just books, it can be individualized, students can have more autonomy and be creative, it's something that they do outside of school anyway so it's something that they know and that relates to their lives outside of school.
Define "effective."	Something students are interested in, that is authentic for them, that they can do.
So really it's engagement in reading that you want to investigate, and technology is just how you want to support or implement this idea, right?	Oh, right—the ideas I just gave are really general ideas about what can engage students (fun, autonomy, chances to be creative, etc) rather than a specific tool to engage them.
Any other important components?	Literacy (reading).
What about literacy is important to your wondering?	What it is about reading in general that discourages or encourages engagement. I guess I mean how students think about literacy/reading.
What **theory or theories** would help explain your components?	Maybe a learning theory that encompasses engagement and/or models of engagement. Something about the components of reading. A model of effective technology use could help frame my methodology by explaining why I'm choosing technology to study engagement.
If you know any of these, what are the components that might matter? (Explain the theories)	Meltzer and Hamann (2004) note three important engagement pieces: 1) Connecting to students' lives 2) Responsive teaching 3) Interaction with people and texts *(continued)*

Guiding Question	Example/Answer
	There's some overlap with Egbert's model of optimal technology-supported learning environments (2004), which has 8 conditions.
	Guthrie and Wigfield (2000) offer a model about reading engagement, too. I'll take it for granted that students will have readings at their level, so I don't have to worry about that important component.
What are the aspects of these theories or models that are directly related to your wondering? (**Theoretical framework**)	I'm not interested in the teacher, really, so I'd say 1) connecting to students' lives and 2) student interaction around text, including time on task, content of interaction. This is where the overlap among the models and theories lies and seems to be important.
What will your research questions be, based on this framework?	How engaged are students in the texts they read, and why do/how do readings connect to students' lives? What kinds of interactions do students have around the texts? How much time on task do they spend, and what is the content of their interaction?
What do you expect to find?	I expect to give a rich description of how these two components (interaction and connection) relate to students' perceptions of their engagement in both specific readings and engagement in reading overall. I expect to be able to say how this framework works or doesn't work in exploring ESL learner reading engagement and suggest how it could be changed.
So what?	A couple things. We'll understand better the importance of connections to ESL students—this hasn't been described in detail before. In addition, we'll see if there are patterns in the interaction that can be related to patterns of engagement. This information should help us not only to develop better reading activities but to investigate the framework components in more depth and work toward a solid theory of reading engagement for ESL learners.

Figure 5.1 Continued

focus the questions, collect and analyze the data, and compare results. The researcher also indicates that the framework will be examined in light of the study results. The examples in this section demonstrate both how researchers create theoretical frameworks and how they use them in their studies.

Bettis and Roe (2008) demonstrate how elements of very different paradigms and theories can be used to form a strong and effective theoretical framework:

> Girls. Reading. Reading girls. Girl power. Instead of posing these ideas as having defined boundaries and unique ideas linked to them, we think they warrant a consolidated consideration. Therefore, we conducted a qualitative study that merges these two bodies of previously separated scholarship ... (p. 1)

> For this inquiry, we employ the theoretical tools of both critical feminism and feminist post-structuralism to help us understand the contradictory space of girlhood and how girls live their lives in classrooms and as readers ... we nestle our study at the juncture of cultural and structural explanations for life in school. (p. 2)

Whether Bettis and Roe's theoretical framework emerges as a "theory" is not the issue. More important is how this integration of theoretical concepts serves as a way for these researchers to develop their investigation in a systematic and understandable way.

Tuzzolino and Armandi (1981) explain the integration of theories that frames their work:

Maslow (1970) categorized human needs into five broad groups, summarized below:

1. Physiological—the fundamentals of survival, including hunger and thirst.
2. Safety—concern over physical survival; ordinary prudence.

3. Affiliation—striving to be accepted by intimate members of one's family or group.
4. Esteem and Status—striving to achieve a high standing relative to others.
5. Self-actualization—a desire to know, understand, systematize, organize, and construct a system of values. (pp. 22–23)

Though originally proposed as a tentative explanation of human motivation warranting further research and testing, most practitioners embraced the theory as a guide for action; in this latter application it has proved quite useful.

Existence-relatedness-growth (ERG) theory (Alderfer, 1972) departs somewhat from Maslow's (Tuzzolino & Armandi, 1981) formulation in placing the source of man's potential in closer interaction with his environment—an open-system thrust. ERG categories include:

Existence: Physiological, Safety (material);
Relatedness: Safety (interpersonal), Belongingness (social);
Esteem Growth: Esteem self-confirmed, self-actualization.

Both models have been used to assess individual need satisfaction in organizations, or to identify organizational settings that would foster such need satisfaction (organizational climate). Additional studies have focused on the nature of prepotency in the hierarchy, on causality, on the validity of the two-tier approach, and so on. These and other research developments, although important, are not our focus here. What is critical is the parallel that might exist between individual and organizational needs, or the potential to analogize using a global construct and integrate such a conceptual framework to CSR (pp. 22–23).

Egbert (2004) combines elements of Flow Theory and theories of second language acquisition to form a model to use as a framework for her study (see Figure 5.2). Using this model, the researcher can clearly see the variables that need to be measured

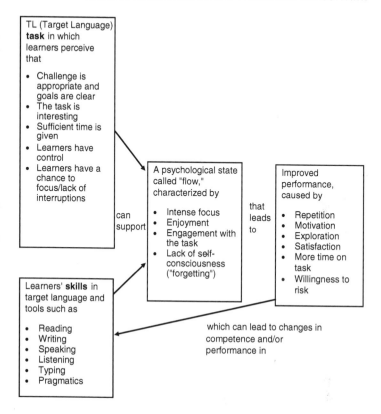

Figure 5.2 The relationship between Flow and language learning. From Egbert (2004).

(components of task and learner skills, elements of Flow, performance indicators), how they might be measured (skills test, student perceptions and/or observations of the task), and what expected outcomes might be (improvement in reading skills).

How Does Theoretical Framework Fit Into the Models?

As indicated in the tree model (see Figure 5.3), the framework arises from the theories that comprise it, and there are an

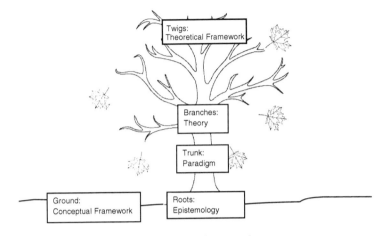

Figure 5.3 Tree diagram for theoretical framework

infinite number of possibilities for different frameworks. The framework then supports the methodology (discussed in the next chapter) and the ways in which the researcher decides to frame it.

In the circle model, it is clear that there is interplay among all of the components of research. This view is less linear than the tree model, but it is similar in the way that it indicates that each component affects the rest of the components in some way (see Figure 5.4).

Conclusion

There is no "correct" theoretical framework for any one study; in fact, a question can be answered from the perspective of any number of theoretical frameworks. However, without a theoretical framework, a study has no reason—it is difficult to understand the decisions that are made and to contextualize the results in any meaningful way. In addition, the theoretical framework results in specific choices for methodology and methods, described in the next chapter.

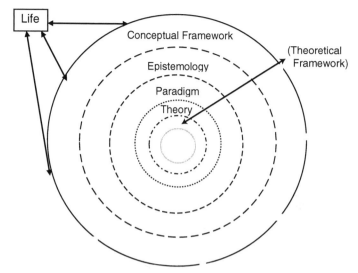

Figure 5.4 Circle diagram for theoretical framework

Guided Practice

1. Review the articles in the appendix for their theoretical framework. What is it? How have the authors explained the connection between the framework and the rest of their study? How does it help you understand the issues involved in the study? Is anything missing? If so, what?

2. Reflect on a study that you hope to conduct. Complete the Guiding Questions table in the appendix for that study. What else do you need to think about before you conduct your research?

Further Reading

Kaplan, A. (1964). *The conduct of inquiry.* San Francisco, CA: Chandler.

Lois Campbell's List of Guidelines for Qualitative Research Studies. Available at http:// qualitativeresearch.ratcliffs.net/loiscampbell.pdf

Rudestam, K., & Newton, R. (1992). *Surviving your dissertation: A comprehensive guide to content and process.* Newberry Park, CA: Sage.

Therborn, G., Chauvel, T., Hout, M., & Kalleberg, A. (2006). *Inequalities of the world: New theoretical frameworks, multiple empirical approaches.* Brooklyn, NY: Verso.

Thomas, R., & Brubaker, D. (2008). *Theses and dissertations: A guide to planning, research, and writing.* New York, NY: Praeger.

References

Alderfer, C. P. (1972). *Existence, relatedness, and growth.* New York, NY: Free Press.

Anfara, V., & Mertz, N. (2006). *Theoretical frameworks in qualitative research.* Thousand Oaks, CA: Sage

Bettis, P., & Roe, M. F. (2008). Reading girls: Living literate and powerful lives. *Research in Middle Level Education Online, 32*(1). Retrieved from http://www.nmsa.org/Publications/RMLEOnline/Articles/Vol32No1/tabid/1749/Default.aspx

blurtit (n.d.). What are the components of theoretical framework? Retrieved from http://www.blurtit.com/q754482.html

Cline, D. (n.d.). Logical structure, theoretical framework. Retrieved from http://education.astate.edu/dcline/guide/framework.html#N_1_

Egbert, J. (2004). A study of Flow Theory in the foreign language classroom. *Canadian Modern Language Review, 60*(5), 549–586.

Egbert, J. (2007). Asking useful questions: Goals, engagement, and differentiation in technology-enhanced language learning. *Teaching English with Technology, 7*(1). Retrieved from http://www.iatefl.org.pl/call/j_article27.htm

Escalada, M. (2009). *Writing the thesis outline: Theoretical framework.* Retrieved from http://devcompage.com

Guthrie, J. T., & Wigfield, A. (2000). Engagement and motivation in reading. In M. L. Kamil, P. B. Mosenthal, P. D. Pearson, & R. Barr (Eds.), *Handbook of reading research: Volume III* (pp. 403–422). New York, NY: Erlbaum.

Herek, G. (1995). Developing a theoretical framework and rationale for a research proposal. In W. Pequegnat & E. Stover (Eds.), *How to write a successful grant application: A guide for social and behavioral scientists* (2nd ed., pp. 137–145). New York, NY: Plenum Press.

Meltzer, J., & Hamann, E. (2004). *Meeting the needs of adolescent English language learners for literacy development and content area learning, Part 1: Focus on motivation and engagement.* Providence, RI: The Education Alliance at Brown University.

Tuzzolino F., & Armandi B. R. (1981). A need-hierarchy framework for assessing corporate social responsibility. *Academy of Management Review, 6*(1), 21–28.

Wiki.answers (n.d.). Retrieved from http://wiki.answers.com/Q/What_is_the_role_of_theoretical_framework_in_research

Zeidler, D. (n.d.). *What is a theoretical framework?: A practical answer.* Retrieved from http://www.coedu.usf.edu/jwhite/secedseminar/theoryframe.pdf

6

RESEARCH METHODOLOGIES AND METHODS: INGREDIENTS FOR RESEARCH SUCCESS

Novice researcher:

> Initially I thought that methodology was just a fancy term for method; I didn't perceive any difference between the two terms in everyday language. However, as is typical in the research world, small differences in words can lead to big variations in research activities. I've discovered that I'm expected to be able to articulate not only the distinctions between the two terms but also the ways that particular methodologies and methods will interact to influence my research work. The good news is that like theoretical frameworks, methodologies and research methods can help to provide a structure for my inquiry. A concern remains, though: How do I choose the ones that will best support my research work?

Experienced researcher:

> *The distinction between methodology and method is a fine one, but it helps novice researchers understand that there are many ways to carry out experiments, case studies, and other methodologies that have specific frames. Too often researchers look for an exact prescription for data collection and analysis strategies when they instead should be able to understand the requirements of the methodology and use the most effective/relevant method for their context. So, while the distinction may be superfluous in the minds of some experienced researchers, it is an important concept for supporting original and useful research and for expanding the boundaries of our methodologies.*

In this chapter, we address the following questions:

- What is a methodology, what is a method, and what is the relationship between the two?
- How do methodologies and methods interact with the other research components?
- What methodologies and methods exist to support research?
- How do methodologies and methods impact a research study?
- How do methodologies and methods fit into the developing models?

REFLECT: What is your understanding of the differences between research methodologies and research methods? What is their impact on each other? What is your understanding of how each impacts a study?

What Are Methodologies and Methods?

In the last several chapters we have explored concepts like epistemology and paradigm that require researchers to reflect on their positionalities, and we have discussed theories and theoretical frameworks that require attention to existing scholarship surrounding research interests. Holding an awareness of these perspectives and understandings will provide a foundation on which to build the next important decision required of a researcher: selecting a methodology and the accompanying methods that will promote information gathering to respond to research questions. How a researcher views knowledge and the possibilities for acquiring it, in addition to the wisdom in the field through which a researcher chooses to view a research question, all lead him or her to begin to draw some conclusions about the best ways to find information concerning a current research topic. When assembled into an organized strategy, these conclusions lead to the methodology, or methodological framework, that a researcher can use to seek answers to research questions. Within that methodology, the researcher uses some specific procedures, or methods, that will perform the actual work of collecting and analyzing the data. We define methodology, then, as **a reasonable plan for gathering and analyzing information that responds to a line of research inquiry**. Methods can be defined as the **specific procedures that accomplish the task of gathering and analyzing the data in a research study**.

The methodology might almost be viewed as a recipe that allows a researcher to cook up findings to feed a research curiosity. Of course, in any meal, decisions are made and circumstances occur that determine the course of the meal preparation. For example, do the cook's background experiences lead to the belief that the meal should be vegetarian? Do allergies preclude the inclusion of certain ingredients in the recipe? Do the diners' tastes necessitate that certain spices be pulled off the shelf? Or do the contents of the kitchen allow or disallow the use of particular utensils? All of these considerations must be included in the formation of a recipe that ends in a suitable result. So it is with decisions that lead to a methodological choice. Instead of things like spices and pots and pans, researchers make decisions about things like who they believe can supply knowledge regarding a research topic and whether that knowledge is certain. They also consider how the knowledge that already exists is relevant and how best to gather new knowledge regarding the topic under discussion. When such decisions are made, the researcher is driven to choose a methodology, such as case study, experiment, or ethnography, that will fit the decision-making that has occurred.

Once a recipe, or methodology, is chosen, even more specific decisions need to be made regarding what tools and procedures, or methods, will result in a positive outcome. Does the recipe in question call for the meat to be baked or broiled or fried? Can a saucepan be used, or will the final product require the use of an oven or a deep fryer to bring out the best flavors? Each recipe requires choices from among a range of options that will allow the chef's knowledge to combine with the ingredients to end in a desirable product. Similarly, within a methodology questions must be answered about which strategies will elicit data that, in the end, addresses the research questions. What sampling method will provide results that allow inferences to be made? Would interviews or surveys—or both—provide the information that prompts a clear understanding of participant perspectives? Which statistical procedures are appropriate? Each strategy is chosen for its ability to best supply data that addresses the research questions; together they form a study's specific research method.

Unlike the contents of a cookbook, however, methodologies cannot be thought of as lists of steps to be applied verbatim to any research situation. Each methodology must be modified to apply appropriately to the topic and in the context required to meet the inquiry. Just as the best chefs use recipes as outlines on which to build their own innovative creations, effective researchers rely on the structure of a methodology to form a study that allows it to satisfactorily address the individual research need. An added pinch of spice here or some extra simmering time there provides each situation with enough of a distinctive twist on the original recipe to meet the unique needs of the current circumstances.

How Do Methodologies and Methods Interact With the Other Research Components?

The researcher's choice of methodology and methods is determined by an integration of the research components discussed in previous chapters and the research topic. A researcher's conceptual framework, epistemology, and paradigm position the researcher to make decisions based on individual beliefs and perspectives. Theories and subsequent theoretical perspectives can act as guiding principles in the formation of a research plan grounded in past scholarship to address current issues. Thus, each of these research components plays a part in allowing the researcher to create a methodology and use methods that are consistent with his or her viewpoint and that will lead to the most reasonable way of gathering information to address the current topic of inquiry.

What Methodologies and Methods Exist to Support Research?

It is helpful to consider some general categories under which lie specific methodologies that might be appropriate for a study. Charles (1998) identifies four basic categories within which most methodologies are situated, and he states that any given investigation falls within the realm of two of these categories. These categories are (1) qualitative, (2) quantitative, (3) experimental, and (4) nonexperimental. Cresswell (2008) explains that qualitative methodologies allow the collection of information that prompts a deeper understanding of some phenomenon; data collected is typically in the form of verbal or written text which is analyzed for patterns and tendencies. Quantitative methodologies, on the other hand, are aimed at collecting information that provides answers to specific questions; participants are often randomly chosen and assigned, and data is numerically based and analyzed statistically.

Often qualitative and quantitative methodologies are viewed as opposites at the epistemic level since qualitative methodologies are considered to involve greater subjectivity on the part of researchers while quantitative methodologies are precipitated on researchers' objectivity and ability to uncover "Truth." These differences stem from researchers' epistemological views and resulting paradigms. In Crotty's (2003) view, however, qualitative and quantitative differences actually lie at the methods level, since it is the ways that data is collected and analyzed rather than a researcher's paradigm that defines these methodologies. He states that either of these methodologies might be called upon depending on the information being sought. Still another view advocates for mixed methods, in which methodologies combine the best of both qualitative and quantitative perspectives in integrating information to address specific circumstances (Maxcy, 2003).

The differences between experimental and nonexperimental research appear to be more clear-cut. Vellutino and Schatschneider (2004) explain that the focus of experimental studies is to apply some treatment to determine if the intervention causes an effect. The goal behind such studies is to establish whether or not there is a cause-and-effect relationship between some variables. Nonexperimental research, on the other hand, is more focused on depicting events, people, and situations as they are (Charles, 1998). While nonexperimental studies might provide for conclusions regarding a correlation between some variables, the **goal** is not on establishing causal relationships (Vellutino &

Schatschneider, 2004), but rather on increasing understanding of a phenomenon.

Following is a brief description of some specific methodologies that lie within these general categories. While space does not permit a complete explanation of all of the components of each methodology, we recommend that you consult some of the many detailed books devoted to each to allow you to make an educated choice regarding the methodology that is most consistent with your research agenda. It is important to keep in mind that while these are explained as separate and distinct, researchers sometimes combine them in creative ways to best tap into the information they seek.

Experiment: As explained above, experimental research examines the connection between two or more variables in order to determine whether a cause-and-effect relationship exists. In a true experimental design, the treatment under investigation is applied randomly to some group, usually a sample of a larger population, and results are compared to a control group that was not subjected to the treatment. A quasi-experimental design also seeks information regarding a cause-and-effect relationship but the treatment is not applied to a group randomly because of some intervening circumstances that cause a random assignment to be unworkable. These might include practical or ethical concerns, such as might exist when working with children in school settings, for example. An experimental methodology might be selected if the researcher values quantitative answers to research questions, and the methodology is typically associated with a positivist approach to a research topic. For more on this methodology, see Campbell and Stanley's (1963) seminal text.

Case study: A case study is research that aims to provide description that enriches understanding about a specific individual, situation, or phenomenon. A primary characteristic of a case study is that it is bounded, which means that a predetermination is made regarding what will be included and excluded from the investigation (Barone, 2004). In other words, a box is drawn around the entity to be studied and a systematic exploration is made of everything that impacts that single bounded system. A case study methodology might be employed if a researcher wants to better understand a behavior or activity in a particular context, with little focus on establishing definitive and replicable truths.

Ethnography: Ethnography is a form of research interested in examining people and their way of life, with a special focus on culture and the ways it impacts meaning-making. Ethnography relies heavily on open-ended forms of participant observation and interviews and privileges active participant interaction and analysis (Anderson-Levitt, 2006). Because of this, it is obvious that an epistemology valuing collaborative knowledge creation is prevalent in ethnographic work. An ethnographic methodology can be used to better understand the ways that people exist within their cultural influences, especially if the group's own perspectives are desired in creating understanding.

Action research: Action research is a systematic application of problem-solving strategies to an authentic question at hand in order to achieve understanding of or resolution to the situation. This cyclical process is typically applied by practitioners of a discipline who recognize a problem, develop a plan to address it, apply the treatment, and then analyze the results (Opie, 2004). The goal is not to add scholarship to the field, although the findings may enrich understanding outside the immediate context. A researcher might employ an action research methodology in the systematic pursuit of a solution to an immediate problem.

After settling on a methodology, the researcher needs to make decisions about which methods to use in choosing participants or events to study, where and when explorations will occur, how information will be collected, and how data will be evaluated to prompt better understanding around the topic in question. Specific methods will be selected by researchers based on their feasibility and their value in gathering and analyzing data. Listed below are some of the many different methods available for use by researchers in pursuit of answers to research questions. Cohen, Manion, and Morrison (2000) define some of these methods as follows:

- *sampling*: choosing a subset of the total population from which the researcher can obtain data;
- *statistical analysis*: applying statistical tests to quantitative data in order to examine patterns or relationships;
- *coding*: organizing qualitative data into themes in order to achieve better understanding of the phenomenon under study or to apply statistical tests;
- *discourse analysis*: exploration of speech or written text, especially as it pertains to social interactions;
- *interview*: interaction in which a researcher asks a participant questions in order to obtain information regarding his or her views on a topic;
- *survey/questionnaire*: instruments through which a researcher gathers data of a descriptive nature or regarding relationships between conditions;
- *observation*: opportunity for the researcher to view a situation in real time;
- *intervention*: an event in which a researcher makes a change to one variable in order to observe the impact on another variable.

How Do the Methodology and Methods Impact a Research Study?

The selection of a methodology is the decision that will guide the remainder of a research study. The principles underlying the methodology will aid in planning for data collection and analysis by prompting the researcher to choose methods consistent with the methodology selected. For example, if the researcher decides that ethnography will provide the kind of information required to respond to the research questions, this decision may lead to the selection of methods like observations or interviews to collect data, followed by analysis using a coding technique (such as that suggested by Boeije, 2010) to find patterns in the qualitative data. The conclusions that can be drawn from this methodology will be different than if an experimental methodology had been used, in which random sampling and statistical analysis might lead the researcher to establish some cause and effect relationships between variables. Table 6.1 demonstrates the relationship between three methodologies and some methods that could be chosen to conduct a study within each. In each example, the method choices reflect some possibilities for a study utilizing that methodology and not a precise recipe to be followed for every study conducted under that methodological umbrella. Methods chosen for a specific study should reflect the needs of the researcher and situation.

Table 6.1 Methodologies and Possible Methods

Experiment	Case Study	Ethnography
• random sample • pre-test/post-test design • survey • inferential statistical analysis	• stratified sample • structured interview • questionnaire • descriptive statistical analysis • coding: progressive reduction	• cluster sample • semi-structured interview • observation • coding: constant comparative analysis

In one example of research in which the choice of methodology has a demonstrated impact on the subsequent outcomes, Lam (2009) presents a case study that demonstrates qualitative data collection and analysis methods:

> For the case study presented in this article, I use the theoretical perspectives discussed above to analyze the ways in which an adolescent girl, who had migrated from China to the United States two years previously, designed her social networks and use of language through her activities on IM with multiple communities across the United States and China. I examine how the youth's literacy practices within these diverse communities are characterized by the synchronic movement across lifeworlds and syncretism in the use of representational resources to (re)define her relations to multiple localities and communities in the process of migration. (p. 380)

> Data for this research are taken from a larger comparative case study of the digital literacy practices of immigrant youth of Chinese descent across transnational contexts. A case-study approach is adopted for this project, with the aim to generate a contextualized analysis of literacy use and learning (Dyson & Genishi, 2005; Erickson, 1986), especially given the paucity of research on immigrant adolescents' practices with digital media. Cases developed from this project examine how the focal adolescents use the Internet to organize social relationships, use and produce information and media content across countries, and develop cross-cultural orientations in their language and literacy learning. The six youths who participated in this project were attending high school in a metropolitan Midwestern city at the time of the study. (p. 381)

> Data collection for this study took place between February 2007 and September 2007 and consisted of home observations of Kaiyee's online literacy practices, semi-structured interviews, screen recordings of her IM exchanges and retrospective reflection on these IM

exchanges with Kaiyee, and selected observations of her activities in her school and the local Chinese immigrant community. (p. 382)

Data analysis involved using qualitative procedures of inductive and interpretive coding, cross-comparison of codes, and triangulation across data (Charmaz, 2006; Coffey & Atkinson, 1996). Analysis was carried out on the data set of interview transcripts, recordings of 600 entries of IM exchanges, and field notes and audiorecorded transcripts from observations. My theoretical perspectives provided an interpretive frame for the development of codes as I related instances in the data to concepts such as social affiliation, design of online networks, social and semiotic resources, hybridity in language use and representation, and mobilizing of resources across networks. (p. 383)

Lam chooses a case study methodology, clearly defining the study by explaining that she will examine the online interactions of a single student. Within this study, Lam utilizes and justifies data collection and analysis methods such as observation, interview, discourse analysis, and various coding schemes to better understand the ways that the student's digital practices contribute to her literacy learning.

McKeown, Beck, and Blake (2009) provide another research example in which their choice of an experimental methodology clearly impacts the performance and outcome of the study. Their methodology is made evident in the explanation of their purpose, in their choice of sampling and data collection methods, and in their conclusions:

The purpose of the study was to compare the effectiveness of two experimental comprehension instructional approaches and a control approach. One experimental approach, the content approach, centered on readers' development of a coherent representation of the text. The other experimental approach, the strategies approach, involved direct teaching of explicit comprehension strategies. The control approach, the basal approach, was based on the instruction presented in the 2003 basal reader that was used in the school district. (p. 223)

Year 2 of the study was designed to replicate our methodology from Year 1, with the addition of random assignment of students to classrooms. We also investigated the effects of the three instructional approaches with expository text and explored transfer to texts that students read without instructional support. Additionally, we included a passage-comprehension baseline test, a pretest in addition to a posttest assessment of strategies use, and teacher exit interviews. (p. 233)

... the content approach showed an advantage over the strategies approach in recall length and quality for narrative texts, but no differences were found for scores on the SVT. Also similar were the results of the lesson-discourse analysis, with content discussion being more focused on text than was strategies discussion and content students providing longer responses than did both strategies and basal-comprehension students. The lesson-discourse analysis included two expository texts that were added for the second year. Similarities were also found in beyond lesson-texts assessments. That is, again, no differences were found among approaches for the comprehension monitoring or the strategies task. (p. 242)

McKeown et al. define their experimental methodology by explaining the study's purpose of comparing experimental and control approaches to comprehension instruction. Some methods they utilize include an experiment, random sampling, discourse analysis, and statistical analysis in attempting to determine which instructional strategy impacted student reading achievement.

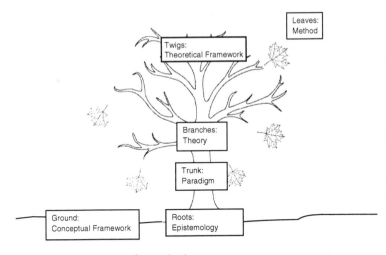

Figure 6.1 Tree diagram for methods

How Do Methodology and Methods Fit Into the Developing Models?

Our tree model (see Figure 6.1) shows the process of conceptualizing a study, acknowledging research components that often go unaddressed but that cannot go untapped. Leaves as a metaphor for methods shows the great range and diversity in methods that is possible for any study and the careful frame that is built underneath the methods so that the most appropriate can be chosen.

In Figure 6.2 (the circles graphic), methodology/method positioned in the center circle points not to its importance but to the number and flow of influences on it.

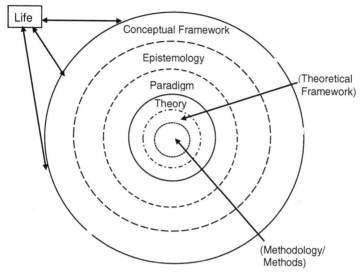

Figure 6.2 Circle diagram for methods

REFLECT: Look back at the graphic that you drew in chapter 1 of your conceptual framework. How would you add the rest of the components so that your overall graphic makes sense to you? Draw it below.

Conclusion

Establishing a methodology early in a research endeavor can be valuable in the ways it provides the researcher with an established framework on which to build a study. Researchers who maintain an awareness of the ways that their theoretical and background knowledge and perspectives lead their research interests can use that awareness to guide their choices regarding the most advantageous plan for their inquiry. A methodology that is consistent with researchers' interests and viewpoints, and methods that promote information gathering and analysis, may make all the difference in the effort to answer important research questions.

Guided Practice

1. Review the articles in the appendix. Describe the methodology/method of each and explain how these relate to the other research components in the study.
2. Consider your own viewpoint on each of the research components discussed thus far, in the context of a potential research question. What methodology seems most consistent with the accumulation of your views? What methods might you use to gather data to respond to your area of inquiry?

Further Reading

Downs, F. (Ed.). (1999). *Readings in research methodology* (2nd ed.). Philadelphia, PA: Lipincott.

Duke, N. K., & Mallette, M. H. (Eds.). *Literacy research methodologies* (2nd ed.). New York, NY: Guilford.

References

Anderson-Levitt, K. M. (2006). Ethnography. In J. L. Green, G. Camilli, & P. B. Elmore (Eds.), *Handbook of complementary methods in education research* (pp. 279–295). Mahwah, NJ: Erlbaum.

Barone, D. M. (2004). Case study research. In N. K. Duke, & M. H. Mallette (Eds.) *Literacy research methodologies* (pp. 7–27). New York, NY: Guilford Press.

Boeije, H. (2010). *Analysis in qualitative research.* Los Angeles, CA: Sage.

Campbell, D., & Stanley, J. (1963). *Experimental and quasi-experimental designs for research.* Independence, KY: Wadsworth.

Charles, C. M. (1998). *Introduction to educational research* (3rd ed.). New York, NY: Longman.

Cohen, L., Manion, L., & Morrison, K. (2000). *Research methods in education* (5th ed.) New York, NY: RoutledgeFalmer.

Cresswell, J. W. (2008). *Educational research: Planning, conducting, and evaluating quantitative and qualitative research* (3rd ed.). Upper Saddle River, NJ: Pearson.

Crotty, M. (2003). *The foundations of social research: Meaning and perspective in the research process.* London, England: Sage.

Dyson, A. H., & Genishi, C. (2005). *On the case: Approaches to language and literacy research.* New York, NY: Teachers College Press.

Erickson, F. (1986). Qualitative methods in research on teaching. In M. Wittrock (Ed.), *Handbook of research on teaching* (3rd ed., pp. 119–161). New York, NY: Macmillan.

Lam, S. E. (2009). Multiliteracies on instant messaging in negotiating local, translocal, and transnational affiliations: A case of an adolescent immigrant. *Reading Research Quarterly, 44*(4), 337–397.

Maxcy, S. J. (2003). Pragmatic threads in mixed methods research in the social sciences: The search for multiple modes of inquiry and the end of the philosophy of formalism. In A. Tashakkori & C. Teddlie (Eds.), *Handbook of mixed methods in social and behavioral research* (pp. 51–90). Thousand Oaks, CA: Sage.

McKeown, M. G., Beck, I. L., & Blake, R. G. K. (2009). Rethinking reading comprehension instruction: A comparison of instruction for strategies and content approaches. *Reading Research Quarterly, 44*(3), 218–253.

Opie, C. (2004). Research approaches. In C. Opie (Ed.), *Doing education research: A guide to first time researchers* (pp. 73–94). London, England: Sage.

Travers, M. (2001). *Qualitative research through case studies.* London: Sage.

Vellutino, F. R., & Schatschneider, C. (2004). Experimental and quasi-experimental design in literacy research. In N. K. Duke & M. H. Mallette (Eds.), *Literacy research methodologies* (pp. 114–148). New York, NY: Guilford.

7

MYTHS AND MISCONCEPTIONS ABOUT RESEARCH

Novice researcher:

> So very, very, very much for the new researcher to learn! Many of the terms and concepts are foreign to the novice or are used in ways that are vastly different from everyday understandings. But being able to speak the language doesn't begin to cover all of the information necessary to conduct a quality research project. Vocabulary, ideas, and views that seem to just roll off the tongue, or pen, of the experienced scholar threaten to drown the newbie in a quagmire of confusion on the path to research wisdom.

Experienced researcher:

> It's a great start if novice researchers understand the definitions of and issues surrounding the theoretical components of research. However, it's just one part of what doing good research entails. There are so many more concepts, ideas, and details to understand—all discussed in different outlets from different perspectives—that they may be difficult for researchers

to sort through. We can point out some of the most common fallacies and provide generic research tips that can point the researcher in the right direction, but what results from any study is up to each individual involved in the process.

In this chapter, we address the following ideas:

- Quantitative and qualitative paradigms and methods do not and cannot mix.
- Never use Wikipedia as a resource.
- Any topic is okay for research.
- Anyone can do research.
- Research takes a lot of time.
- You can learn to do research just by reading.
- All you need to do statistics is the right software.
- Any research that is published is good research.
- Qualitative research is never generalizable.
- Short-term research is as good as longer term research.
- Research is important in and of itself—it doesn't need to be applied.
- Statistics are hard to understand.
- One study is enough for us to say "research says.…"
- What is important is that you did your best.

REFLECT: Which of the above do you think are myths and which advice? Why?

Bercovitz (1986) notes that research can have "tremendous value and it can also be nearsighted, overestimated, abused, or misused … and too frequently misunderstood or undervalued" (p. 414). This book is an attempt to understand some of the terms used in research. It is a small start toward helping to not only avoid misunderstanding but to emphasize the value of research when it is conducted rigorously and thoughtfully. The ideas in this final chapter add to that attempt—they have been collected from students, faculty, and the literature. Although they may seem rather random, these are ideas that arise frequently and play a central role in much research. Again, we include the caveat that there is more than one perspective on each of these ideas that the researcher can consider.

Quantitative and Qualitative Paradigms and Methods Do Not and Cannot Mix

Although many researchers believe that there is a clear line between qualitative and quantitative research (the "incompatibility thesis"), according to Onwuegbuzie and Leech (2005) and Salomon (2006), this distinction is often a spurious one. In fact, some methodologies require that both be considered, e.g., single subjects research. Mixed methods research, or multimethodology, is explained by the *compatibility thesis* and has become more accepted as researchers attempt to increase rigor and plausibility by triangulating data. Regardless of perspective, researchers must decide for themselves if the arguments they make in favor of their method are sound and then provide an argument for the reader that demonstrates why this is so.

Never Use Wikipedia as a Resource

Many high schools and universities have banned the use of Wikipedia as a citation source, but not as a resource, for research papers and other academic work. However, Perrin (1987) notes that we should "look everywhere and explore every potential source of information" (p. 51). That does not mean that any resource is acceptable as evidence or that some sources are not more credible than others, but that any source can prod researchers in a new direction, provide references to seminal publications, or send them to additional sources. Using Wikipedia is an easy way to access general ideas, definitions, and related ideas and can facilitate finding primary, credible sources for information.

Any Topic Is Okay for Research

Some topics are "just not worth the time" (Perrin, 1987, p. 53). This includes those on which there is no new angle, that have no meaning outside of the researcher's life, or that are so broad that the questions cannot possibly be addressed in one study. Good topics are those, then, on which the researcher can shed some new light, that are based on pressing needs, and that the researcher is invested enough in to carry out the work and do it well.

Anyone Can Do Research

It takes skills, training, and resources to do high-quality research (Perrin, 1987; Vickers, 2008). Often not even those who are supposedly trained to do research can put together a study that is both rigorous and meaningful. That does not mean that the attempt should not be made, but that collaboration, practice, and lots of reading go far toward developing good researchers.

Research Takes a Lot of Time

Pannbacker and Middleton (1991–92) note that "Many productive researchers have no more free time or no fewer commitments than those who do not engage in research. Instead, those who do research simply make the time to do it. It is a matter of prioritizing and managing time. Like anything else, with practice comes efficiency" (p. 128). Time depends on the size and type of study, the number of participants and data sources, and the techniques for analysis used. The authors note that computers can help, from preparing reports to supporting data analysis, increasing accuracy, and helping record references. Researchers can learn time-saving strategies from peers and texts but should also be careful in taking shortcuts that impact the rigor of the study.

You Can Learn To Do Research by Reading

Like learning to ride a bicycle or barbecue a steak to perfection, conducting good research cannot be learned only from a book. As noted in many places in this volume, reading is a good and necessary start, but novice researchers need to practice and work with good, experienced researchers. In addition, they need to be exposed to many different kinds of research practice (Pannbacker & Middleton, 1991-92); this includes work with the responsible conduct of research.

"All You Need To Do Statistics Is the Right Software" (Vickers, 2008, p. 85)

The wrong statistical analysis, even when run well, can break a study. Inputting data into the computer and running an ANOVA at the click of a mouse does not mean that the resulting statistics will provide evidence to support the research questions. Statistics is a specialization that requires intensive study and an in-depth knowledge of both why and how. Vickers notes that it behooves any researcher to make friends with a statistician who also has some knowledge of the researcher's work.

Any Research That Is Published Is Good Research

Davis (2007) comments that "The literature is rife with half-truths, popular myths, contradictions, poorly designed studies, misinterpreted findings, and conclusions soaked in the personal biases and deeply held assumptions of researchers" (p. 572). Care needs to be taken not to overstate the importance of findings or ignore contradictory findings, to explicitly state the researcher's assumptions and biases, and to use appropriate statistical procedures. Published research has both limitations and weaknesses (Pannbacker & Middleton, 1991–92). Not all journals publish studies of the same quality and have the same review process and standards of rigor. Researchers can become familiar with the questions that journals use for evaluating research and can peruse research forums that explicitly analyze research studies. In addition, reviewing the references used in a study, analyzing the theoretical framework and its use, and following other suggestions that Ryan (2005) offers can help readers determine whether a study constitutes "good" research.

Qualitative Research Is Never Generalizable

Davis (2007) and others note that rigorous, relevant, and systematic qualitative research can indeed be generalized to larger populations, but that usually qualitative methodology is used in a more descriptive, meaning-seeking way that looks at a specific phenomenon. Researchers using a qualitative methodology need to consider carefully whether there is reason and evidence to claim greater generalizability. For example, self-reports alone of "experiences, judgments, and perceptions of reality" (Davis, p. 57) do not typically allow for generalizability. Arguments for and against the generalizability of qualitative research abound, both on the Web and in journal forums, and researchers can acquaint themselves with these arguments in their quest to settle this argument in their own minds.

Short-Term Research Is as Good as Longer Term Research

Davis (2007) decries researchers' "hit and run" tactics where they jump from study to study or place to place, neglect context, and ignore the input of practitioners who can make an important contribution. Egbert, Huff, McNeil, Preuss, and Sellen (2009) agree that it takes time and context to understand patterns and environments and that practitioners must be consulted, regardless of the paradigm through which the research is viewed. The more time spent in a place or with a phenomenon, the better the understanding of it can be.

Research Is Important In and Of Itself—It Doesn't Need To Be Applied

Davis (2007) also laments the gap between research and the people to whom it can make a difference. He notes the academic language that keeps lay people in most fields from accessing the research and the continued support in research areas for "pure" science without application. Davis believes that "Conscientious scholars can and should write to be understood" (p. 571). Daniel (1996) claims, however, that there has not been enough emphasis on basic research and there is a distinct lack of theoretical grounding in many studies that must be developed before it can be applied. Clearly, both basic ("pure") and applied science have their uses.

Statistics Are Hard To Understand

When they are hidden inside academic jargon and obfuscating text, it is probably true that statistics are difficult to comprehend for many consumers of research. In fact, the reader's ignorance of statistics can make it easier for unwarranted claims to go unchallenged. It is the researcher's job to make sure that the reader can understand the study design, the use of statistics, and the specific procedures and also to describe how they are not only appropriate but useful in the study. On the other hand, those who read, use, and analyze research should make it a point to acquaint themselves with at least the most common procedures so that they can recognize and analyze the study in a meaningful way.

One Study Is Enough for Us To Say "Research Says ..."

Unfortunately, the popular press, administrators and legislators, and professionals in a variety of fields are often looking for evidence to support their positions, and one study is often reported as conclusive support. Researchers have a duty to show readers why more research is needed and what kind it might be; this is the purpose of the "implications" section of the research report.

"What Is Important Is That You Did Your Best" (Vickers, 2008, p. 85)

This statement may be true in baking and marathons, but bad research for any reason can do more harm than good. According to Vickers (2008), the research is not about the researcher; it should be about the passion that the researcher has to make a difference as a result of the research. That means that the research is done well according to norms, standards, and logic; these do not always equate with a researcher's best.

Conclusion

As we have said throughout, the ideas in this text are presented from our point of view and should appropriately be given more thought and discussion. However, we do believe that the underlying notion that having a specific way to frame and talk about research components is essential. Doing rigorous, effective, and useful research is not easy, and starting from a solid foundation of understanding can help researchers, both novice and experienced, to provide the consistency and access needed to move the research endeavor forward.

Guided Practice

1. Look through research studies conducted by novice and experienced researchers. Can you find any instances of the researchers adhering to some of the myths and/or advice above? What difference does it make in their studies?
2. Think about a study that you plan to conduct. What more

do you need to find out about the issues in this chapter? Find resources that help understand them more deeply and share them with your peers.

Further Reading

Brannen, J. (2005). Mixing methods: The entry of qualitative and quantitative approaches into the research process. *International Journal of Social Research Methodology, 8*, 173–184.

References

Bercovitz, A. (1986). All you ever wanted to know about research but were afraid to ask. *AAZPA Annual Proceedings.* 414–416. Available from http://library.sandiegozoo.org/zoopubs_nav/b.html

Daniel, L. (1996). Kerlinger's research myths. *Practical Assessment, Research, and Evaluation, 5*(4). Retrieved from http://pareonline.net/getvn.asp?v=5&n=4

Davis, S. (2007). Bridging the gap between research and practice: What's good, what's bad, and how can one be sure? *Phi Delta Kappan*, April, 569–578.

Egbert, J., Huff, L., McNeil, L., Preuss, C., & Sellen, J. (2009). Pedagogy, process, and classroom context: Integrating teacher voice and experience into research on technology-enhanced language learning. *Modern Language Journal, 93*, 754–768.

Onwuegbuzie, A., & Leech, N. (2005). Taking the "Q" out of research: Teaching research methodology courses without the divide between quantitative and qualitative paradigms. *Quality and Quantity, 39*, 267–296.

Pannbacker, M., & Middleton, G. (1991–92). Common myths about research. *National Student Speech Language Hearing Association Journal, 19*, 128–137.

Perrin, R. (1987). Myths about research. *The English Journal, 76*(7), 50–53.

Ryan, G. (2005). What are standards of rigor for qualitative research? *Workshop on Interdisciplinary Standards for Systematic Qualitative Research*. Washington, DC, National Science Foundation. Retrieved from http://www.wjh.harvard.edu/nsfqual/Ryan%20Paper.pdf

Salomon, G. (2006). The systemic vs. analytic study of complex learning environments. In J. Ellen & R. E. Clark (Eds.), *Handling complexity in learning environments: Theory and research* (pp. 255–274). Amsterdam, The Netherlands: Elsevier.

Vickers, A. (2008). A basic introduction to research: How not to do research. *Journal of Social Integrative Oncology, 6*(20), 82–85.

Appendices

Appendix A: Guiding Questions Worksheet

Appendix B: Articles

Article 1

Egbert, J., & Salsbury, T. (2009). "'Out of complacency and into action": An exploration of professional development experiences in school/home literacy engagement. *Teaching Education, 20*(4), 375–393. Reprinted by permission of the publisher.

Article 2

Bettis, P., & Roe, M. (2008). Reading girls: Living literate and powerful lives. *Research in Middle Level Education Online, 32*(1), 1–18. Reprinted by permission of the publisher.

Article 3

Norrish, H., Farringdon, F., Bulsara, M., & Hands, B. (2012). The effect of school uniform on incidental physical activity among 10-year-old children. *Asia-Pacific Journal of Health, Sport and Physical Education, 3*(1), 51–63. Reprinted by permission of the publisher.

GUIDING QUESTIONS WORKSHEET

A. **Guiding Question**	**Example/Answer**
What's your topic?	
What is it that you wonder?	
Why do you wonder this?	
What specifically do you want to find out?	
Why is this important?	
What are the main components of your question that you need to find out about?	
Any other important components?	

What **theory or theories** would help explain your components?

If you know any of these, what are the components that might matter? (Explain the theories)

What are the aspects of these theories or models that are directly related to your wondering? (**Theoretical framework**)

What will your research questions be, based on this framework?

How will you find the answers to your questions?

What do you expect to find?

So what?

ARTICLE 1: "OUT OF COMPLACENCY AND INTO ACTION": AN EXPLORATION OF PROFESSIONAL DEVELOPMENT EXPERIENCES IN SCHOOL/HOME LITERACY ENGAGEMENT

Authors: Joy Egbert; Tom Salsbury
Affiliation: Department of Teaching and Learning, Washington State University, Pullman, USA
Published in: *Teaching Education*, Volume 20, Issue 4, December 2009, pages 375–393.

Abstract

Parents can provide interaction that is crucial to student learning. Helping teachers connect students' home and school lives and assisting parents in understanding possible roles in student learning can contribute to student achievement. A one-year funded project focused on: (1) helping teachers involve parents in the literacy achievement of their children; (2) developing responsible, effective, technologically enhanced partnerships between teachers and parents; and (3) providing a model for professional development in home/school literacy connections. This article explains the research base and procedures for the project, outcomes that impact how parent-teacher engagement can be formed, examples of effective activities, and guidelines for teacher educators to promote successful professional development in home/school engagement.

Keywords: engagement; literacy; parents; professional development

I do not think that my parents and teachers should talk about my grades because they are trying to teach us to be independent so we should have to deal with this on are [sic] own also parents do not know about your class life and they do not know how the class is structured. (Fifth-grade student)

This student raises several issues about parent and teacher communication, including its focus, purpose, and possibilities. These, and other parent-teacher issues, are important because, without doubt, family involvement in a child's schooling can result in higher achievement for that child (Epstein et al., 2002; Rudney, 2005). More specifically, home literacy experiences can have a positive impact on student literacy achievement (August & Shanahan, 2006). In addition, students and schools can benefit from the knowledge brought to school by parents and families (August & Shanahan, 2006; Epstein, 1996; Nathenson-Mejia, 1994; Valdes, 1996).

Despite their importance to schooling, parents are not tapped often enough even though they can provide interaction that is crucial to student learning. Parents may be underutilized in part because many teachers are concerned about time, language, culture, and social barriers in forging relationships with parents, and parents may be unaware or unsure of what their role in school should be. Helping teachers to connect students' home and school lives and assisting parents in understanding possible roles in school can contribute not only to student achievement but also to a greater sense of community for all participants.

In order to explore these issues and seek possible solutions, a one-year project focusing on parent involvement was funded by the Washington State Higher Education Coordinating Board. The project involved teachers from three geographically and demographically diverse school districts and faculty from a state university. The project goals were threefold: (1) to help teachers involve parents in the literacy achievement of their children; (2) to develop responsible, effective, technologically enhanced partnerships between teachers and parents; and (3) to provide a model for professional development in home/school literacy connections.

The project centered on understanding challenges that teachers face in partnering with parents and the types of home/school connections that are essential in establishing school community. At the same time, this project emphasized literacy strategies that teachers and parents could use to reach all students to support literacy across the content areas. The project activities took place in classrooms with school-based teacher cohorts and in homes with parents and children. Faculty encouraged and supported teachers as the teachers presented partnership opportunities and experiences for the professional development of their colleagues and worked within schools and districts to further develop materials and ideas for effective tasks.

This article presents the research base and procedures for the project, outcomes that impact how parent-teacher engagement can be formed, examples of activities that teachers found effective, and guidelines for teacher educators to promote successful professional development in home/school engagement.

Research Bases

Below we discuss two focal research foundations for the project: (1) situated learning, which is the basis for the design of teacher development assignments that take place in authentic contexts; and (2) scaffolded reading experiences, which focus on pre-, during-, and post-reading activities and can facilitate student literacy achievement. We also briefly describe the research behind interactive homework, a format that teachers adopted with success during the project described in this paper.

Teacher Development Through Situated Learning

In order to create effective learning opportunities for teachers, it is crucial to understand how and why teachers learn. Research on teacher learning, including situated learning, forms the first research base for this project.

Most researchers agree that teacher learning combines a mix of content, task, and dispositional knowledge. In addition, learning to teach requires that teachers transfer course content to school settings across contexts, and that teachers continue to learn and grow as practicing professionals (Andersen, Reder, & Simon, 1996; Griffin, 1995; Hendricks, 2001). Learning to teach requires understanding how to draw on content, task, and dispositional knowledge to deal with authentic classroom dilemmas spontaneously, or to employ "thinking-in-action" (Schon, 1987). McMeniman and Evans (1998, p. 1) conclude that teachers change their practices and beliefs (or "learn") when "presented with evidence that shows positive effects of the new teaching method on quality of learning outcomes" and "develop expertise in the new method," and this is also true for other practices such as partnering with families. The results of the Findings on Learning to Teach study (NCRTL, 1994, p. 2) support the idea that teachers need to "learn to think strategically about learners" in specific contexts and in relation to specific content.

As these references to existing scholarship suggest, coursework alone, devoid of the opportunities to practice, challenge assumptions, apply ideas that are new to them, and see evidence of student improvement, may lead to theoretical knowledge about teaching—what Kennedy (1999) calls expert knowledge, but not craft knowledge. As Kennedy explains, expertise arises from the joining of expert and craft knowledge (this is called "pedagogical content knowledge" by Shulman, 1987, and others).

We see situated learning as a way to help teachers understand some of the challenges they face, produce, and consider alternatives for working with parents, and collaborate as they reflect on new practices such as the use of technology to partner with constituents outside of the school building. In other words, teacher change and growth occur through learning that is situated in classrooms (Brown, Collins, & Duguid, 1989; Feiman-Nemser & Remillard, 1996; Lave & Wenger,

1991; Putnam & Borko, 2000). Herrington and Oliver (2000) provide a useful framework for professional development based on situated learning principles. This framework includes the following elements of situated learning:

- provide authentic contexts that reflect the way the knowledge will be used in real life;
- provide authentic activities;
- provide access to expert performances and the modeling of processes;
- provide multiple roles and perspectives;
- promote reflection and articulation;
- provide for authentic assessment of learning within the tasks.

This framework provided support and guidance for the conduct of the project outlined further below. Unfortunately, most professional development projects for teachers do not include these elements.

Teaching Reading to All Students: Scaffolded Reading Experiences

The second research foundation in this project supports the use of scaffolded reading experiences (SREs) for all students across content areas. There are many studies that indicate the longstanding history of research that supports selected components of SREs (cf., Beck, McKeown, Sinatra, & Loxterman, 1991; Droop & Verhoeven, 1998; Englert, Tarrant, Mariage, & Oxer, 1994; Fisher, 1994; Palincsar & Brown, 1984). Building on the work of Fitzgerald and Graves (2004), scaffolded reading experiences provide an instructional base for the project. In this approach, teachers establish before-, during-, and after-reading activities that match the needs of specific learners. These decisions on how to frame and use these activities demand expertise and informed decision-making by teachers, but they can be carried out in part by children with the support of family members. For example, a teacher might employ a graphic organizer to help a student understand the events of a narrative and then have the student explain the story to a family member using the organizer. One intention of this project was to reinforce teachers' pedagogical content knowledge in using SREs

(Kennedy, 1999; Shulman, 1987) and to extend this knowledge to help teachers involve parents in the literacy learning of their children. Although this approach is becoming more common, it is not often a focus of professional development experiences in situated contexts.

Interactive Homework

Another goal of the project was to help teachers tie reading scaffolds to homework tasks in which parents could have a small but crucial role. This type of homework task is known as interactive homework, or "homework assignments that require students to talk to someone at home about something interesting that they are learning in class" (Epstein et al., 2002, n.p.). Quasi-experimental research (e.g., Epstein, Simon, & Salinas, 1997; Epstein & Van Voorhis, 2001; Van Voorhis, 2001) has found that interactive homework that involved parents resulted in higher grades, higher achievement, and better attitudes on the part of learners. Perhaps as important, interactive homework helps establish links between parents and teachers that make interactions easier and perceptions more transparent.

The features of interactive homework include:

- teachers guide involvement and interaction;
- parents do not "teach"—students are responsible for learning and sharing;
- parents interact with children in new ways;
- teachers show children that they understand the importance of family interaction;
- tasks are engaging and challenging;
- interactive homework is assigned two to four times per month, with the expectation for family interaction of 10-15 minutes per task, and two to three days may be given for completion;
- tasks are content- and language-based, relevant, interactive, and written in simple language;
- teachers provide follow up and student sharing.

Readings on the benefits of interactive homework were included in the reading packet provided for teachers in this project (the reading list is available in Appendix A). However, specific tasks were not provided for the teachers, as we were interested not only in discovering their processes of learning but also fitting the homework tasks to their specific contexts. Therefore, we evaluated the teachers' development of awareness and tasks over time, rather than looking at their adherence to a prescribed set of criteria.

Overall, the emphasis of this project on teacher learning in situated contexts with specific focus on literacy connections for *all* students/parents provides both a much-needed explanation of how such effective professional development experiences might occur and an overview of useful home/school interactions.

Method

Participants and Tasks

In order to meet the objectives of the project, we worked with teacher volunteers in our three partner districts, which were geographically dispersed across the east side of the state. The teachers met one or more of three criteria: they had either (1) taken a web-based graduate level course called "Reading across the curriculum," which focused on the use of scaffolded reading experiences; (2) participated in the dissemination/professional development projects that resulted from this course; or (3) had a school plan focused on reading. In addition, one administrator from each district agreed to participate, although not all did so actively. The first district ("North"), in a fairly remote and rural area of the state, enrolled fewer than 2000 students but had a large minority population consisting of Native American (33%) and Hispanic (14%) students. In this district, 47% of the students received free or reduced lunch and 3.7% were receiving English as a Second Language (ESL) services. One first-grade teacher, one fifth-grade teacher, the high-school ESL teacher, and one principal from the North district participated in the project. In the second, suburban district ("Middle"), 4250 students were enrolled, 46% of whom received free or reduced lunch, 11% identified themselves as a minority, and 2.9% received ESL services. Four teachers from the same elementary school, the librarian, and the principal participated in this project. The third district ("South"), the largest in the state in area, enrolled over 13,000 students, 28% of whom received free or reduced lunch, 12% identified themselves as minority, and 4% received ESL services. Six teachers from the same elementary school participated in the project. In total, one librarian, two building principals, and 14 K-12 classroom teachers completed the project.

One university faculty member was assigned to each district and traveled to meet with the teachers to collaborate on outlining specific challenges to partnering with their students' parents. In between visits, all faculty and teachers interacted through a university-based electronic discussion forum. Briefly, the project activities included the following:

1. During the first semester of the project, in face-to-face meetings with teachers, faculty members reviewed the literature and brainstormed ways to work with parents. The faculty encouraged teachers to focus on connecting with students and parents, working with student interests, and making sure assignments fit into home lives. These discussions continued among all participants in an electronic discussion forum.

2. Beginning late in the first semester and continuing throughout the second semester of the project, each teacher-participant created five literacy-based assignments for their students and parents to scaffold in-class reading; some of the tasks were collaborations among teachers. These were posted in the electronic discussion forum so that all participants could read and comment on the assignments and related discussion items.

3. Faculty and teachers worked together to choose resources that would support the special needs of their schools, parents, and students. Several of the tasks were delayed due to problems with the resources either being delivered late or not working properly. Among the resources were digital audio recorders, video recorders, LeapPads (LeapFrog, Inc.), bilingual books, and electronic translators. The resources were put to immediate use in the tasks.

4. Teacher disseminations of project information and/or results included reading groups, demonstrations, parent nights, and meetings. Some of them lasted up to a day, others for several months.

Several teacher-participants also traveled to the university to interact with preservice teachers around project issues.

The project activities contained the elements of situated learning as outlined in Table 1.

Data Sources and Analysis

Participants posted 87 printed pages of comments/discussion with an average of five posts on each page to the discussion forum. (This total does not include additional attachments such as examples of projects, photos, and resource lists that were used as supplemental data.) In order to evaluate the project, the authors were guided by Bogdan and Biklen's (2003) and Creswell's (2003) coding schemes. The authors read the data from the asynchronous electronic discussion forum for salient themes and sub-themes. Initial themes were "perceptions" and "strategies," and sub-themes included initial perceptions, ongoing perceptions, concerns/barriers, activity ideas, uses of technology, reasons for success, and the future. These formed the framework for more detailed coding to assign specific instances and examples to each theme. As the coding progressed, some of the themes were integrated, while others were divided into further sub-themes. Survey data from pre- and post-project surveys of teachers, parents, and students, by nature already categorized, were analyzed in light of their relationships to the discussion coding categories. Meeting notes and other anecdotes were used to supplement and triangulate the data coding. Overall, this process allowed us to evaluate the project through understanding the process, teacher perceptions and changes, and outcomes.

Results and Discussion

Initial Perceptions

Teachers

At the face-to-face meetings at the start of the project and in the pre-project survey, most teachers voiced general frustration with trying unsuccessfully to make connections with some of the parents of their students, regardless of economic or language status. Several teachers noted the low return rate of current home activities (receiving five out of 25 assignments was a recurrent event). While one teacher claimed that "parents make a lot of promises, but do not follow through on these," another noted that "home life is better or worse for kids and parents" and that this impacts what parents can do at home. Teachers understood that parents have many responsibilities and barriers to school participation, just as they felt barriers to working closely or spending extra time trying to communicate with parents. Most of the teachers commented that they had not had any real training in how to work with parents successfully. The overall feeling at the beginning of the project was one of past frustration and hopeful expectation that this project could help with the parent-teacher connection.

Table 1 Project Activities Alignment with Situated Learning Elements

Situated learning element	Project activity
Provide authentic context that reflects the way the knowledge will be used in real life	The context was the teachers' own classrooms. They worked with colleagues within their schools and districts and with other teachers throughout the state who were facing the same issues. Each individual task was created based upon the school curriculum for the specific grade level and the state standards for literacy and content-learning.
Provide authentic activities	Activities for the teachers included reading and discussion, creating student tasks, assessing, and reflecting—all central to teachers' classroom lives.
Provide access to expert performances and the modeling of processes	University faculty worked as facilitators and encouragers so that teachers/schools could find ways that suited their own contexts. Through two to three face-to-face meetings and consistent interaction within the electronic discussion forum, faculty provided constant advice and support of all kinds.

Situated learning element	Project activity
Provide multiple roles and perspectives	Teachers shared their thoughts and experiences via an electronic discussion system. Each district noted the individual complexities that they were dealing with and compared and contrasted those with teachers in the other districts.
Promote reflection and articulation	Collaborative groupings of teachers, a complex task, and opportunities to publicly present successes and failures promoted both reflection and articulation within the electronic discussion. Participant contact averaged 80 hours over the project year, including face-to-face visits, email exchanges and phone calls, and electronic forum discussions. Teacher participants made 319 total entries in the discussion forum, and many more were made by faculty. This is an average of 19 postings per teacher-participant. In addition, teacher-participants made 564 viewings of postings, an average of 33 per teacher participant. This clearly shows not only active involvement but constant interaction among participants.
Provide for authentic assessment of learning within the tasks	Teachers evaluated both their students' outcomes and their own pedagogical decisions. Faculty collected parent, teacher, and student surveys (see Appendix B for the teacher survey form), emails, and meeting notes, and the electronic forum data to use in evaluating the project. A follow-up survey was also administered to teachers during the semester following the end of the project.

Parents and Students

The surveys, also completed by approximately 50% of the parents and all of the teachers' students, indicated some additional interesting trends and concerns. For example, more than two-thirds of the students said that teachers and parents communicated, but many others indicated that they did not know whether their teachers communicated with their parents and that they did not know the content when they did. Across classes, students believed that practice helps students become better readers, and they commented consistently that teachers and parents could help students read better by making them practice more. Parents, however, indicated that reading progress comes from "making it fun," "understanding better," "helping find a book that captures their interest," and "relating the material to their lives."

While the majority of parents believed that reading progress is seen through increased interest, students thought that reading faster and spelling better, as demonstrated by better grades, were the important indicators. All parents felt that teachers were helping their children learn to read, although one parent commented: "The reading logs are a pain and I see very little value. The students shouldn't be graded on how well organized the parents are." In addition, although a majority of parents felt that email was a good way to communicate with teachers, all but one teacher felt that writing individual emails was too time-consuming. Furthermore, several teachers noted that parents were interested only in the outcomes or products of instruction, but the parents who responded to the survey indicated that they desired to know about how they could volunteer, special projects that they could help with, and insight into the child that parents may not discover at home. Responses by parents to ideal communication with teachers ranged widely, from "Having access to a live video camera would help us see our child's behavior during class" to "2-WAY. I not only get info from the teacher, but have an opportunity to communicate our needs as well," and "getting weekly newsletters" to "only through conferences."

From these data we can determine several possible areas of need. First, parents, teachers, and students need to have some common understandings about reading and literacy. Second, parents, like their children, have different needs to be met. Third, communication between parents and teachers can help teachers understand these needs; in addition, this communication should be as transparent as possible to students.

Ongoing Themes

Relevant themes that arose from the data include: (1) concerns/barriers; (2) activity ideas; (3) uses of technology; (4) reasons for success;

and (5) the future. Although the volume of data limits their presentation here, the comments excerpted in this section help frame the project from the teachers' points of view. Findings for each of the themes are presented below.

Concerns/Barriers

Throughout the project, teachers looked for ways to connect with parents. They discovered that some of their concerns were not justified and that there were barriers that they had not thought of previously. Interaction with faculty and other teachers often helped overcome these barriers. Teacher comments about barriers centered on three issues: parent interest, connections, and time.

Interest

One teacher who was sending home a reading log that parents were supposed to sign found that some students were forging their parents' signatures, and others just did not turn in the assignments. The teacher reflected that, because parents were not involved in the task, they were not invested enough to care about it. Similarly, teachers noticed when the homework task was not working, that it often had to do with both student and parent interest. One teacher noted: "I think that having to write a paragraph was an assignment that they did not want to do." This teacher commented that more successful assignments were those that were geared more toward parent-student interaction. One teacher decided to do "something so totally fun and different, parents might get more involved."

Other teachers mentioned that the seeming lack of parent interest may have resulted from parents not knowing what they were supposed to do exactly. Several teachers attributed the lack of returned, completed assignments, particularly reading logs, to this. Teachers were discouraged with this situation at first, particularly when they felt that they had put a lot of time and effort into the assignment. Discussion revolved around simplifying content and inciting greater parent interest in the assignments. This was successful in several ways, as noted later in this article.

Connections

Teachers struggled at times to make connections with parents in their home assignments. Several teachers noted religious and cultural barriers. For example, in one district, there was a group of parents who did not use or approve of technology of any kind, including movies, music, TV, and even some books. Faculty and teacher participants advised that focusing on more content-based print resources might work to connect with these parents. In addition, several teachers noted that a group of their students were not allowed to participate in science fiction or fantasy tasks during a unit using "*A wrinkle in time*" (L'Engle, 1973) and looking at various conceptions of space.

In other homes, parents did not allow their children to speak English at home and would not participate in homework from the public school. Other language minority parents thought that it was the teachers' job to help with homework. Some of these and other parents in the districts were also hesitant to sign student papers for a variety of reasons. Teachers agreed that they needed to work on increasing the trust level with these parents.

Activity Ideas

The Roles of Time and Simplicity

Time played a major role in successful parent-teacher connections. Teachers noted that there were always parents who did not seem to (or told the teachers that they did not) want to take the time to sit down with their children. As the project went on, teachers became more focused on literacy tasks that were not as time-consuming, that required parent input to complete, and that were better integrated into the curriculum. They were more concerned with effective tasks that were not offensive to any particular group and with trying to understand the parents' needs. One effective activity was as simple as having students put together a family tree with their parents. The teacher noted:

> The most delightful thing was that Maria came up to me after class the next day and spread out a beautiful family tree she had made with

her parents' help. What blew my mind was that she went back four or five generations. It was amazingly symmetrical and complete.

Another activity described by a first-grade teacher built on family history and family dynamics through the telling of fairytales. The children looked at several different versions of common fairy tales and then shared those tales with family members at home. Older family members then shared a fairytale that they liked when they were children. The first-graders drew pictures to illustrate the fairytale they had heard at home, and many of the children invited their parents or grandparents to the class for a play involving fairy tales. Family partners were able to participate in the activity regardless of language background, skill level, or time availability.

At the beginning of the project some teachers expressed frustration at the small number of homework activities that students completed, and they were concerned about assigning time-consuming homework that involved parents. One sixth-grade teacher who had had many difficulties getting assignments back simplified and got very creative. She had students find a photo (or take one themselves) that represented a form of government that they had studied in class. Using the WordArt function of Microsoft Word and their photos, they created a short quiz for their parents. The parents were to guess which form of government each photo represented. The teacher described the quiz as a "simple, fun activity that the kids were proud of making" and consequently proud to show their parents. She also reported that most students turned in the assignments with "comments galore" from the parents.

The Role of Discussion

When teachers started posting these successes to the electronic discussion, other teachers used similar principles of interactive homework to create tasks. For example, one teacher sent home fact and opinion articles as springboards to deeper discussions with family members about "slanted" media and perspective. Discussions with family members characterized many of the activities. One child reported to her teacher that her father had become so interested in the unit on weather (through family discussion about climate in his home country with the aid of bilingual picture dictionaries) that the child's father bought a thermometer specifically to record daily temperatures for the homework. Another teacher had her children find a picture of a parent or other family partner with a "bad hair day" or a hairstyle of the past. The picture served as a prompt to an interview with parents over past hairstyles. The children interviewed their family partners about past hairstyles. After the interview, the students wrote a paragraph using the interview questions and included the original picture as an illustration to their written work.

Teachers Involve Parents in Schoolwork (TIPS)

The lead author of this project introduced the teachers to pre-made interactive homework assignments called TIPS (Teachers Involve Parents in Schoolwork, National Network of Partnership Schools; see http://www.csos.jhu.edu/P2000/tips/index.htm). Several teachers expressed enthusiasm for the TIPS activities. For example, one first-grade teacher described a TIPS activity that called for family involvement in learning common and proper nouns. In this activity, the student and the family partner work independently to make a list of proper nouns from a provided list of common nouns (e.g., the Sears Tower for the common noun "skyscraper"). The child and family partner compared lists and discussed differences. The activity was then modified whereby the child provided one common noun from a list of five proper nouns that the family partner created. The first-grade teacher who described the activity reported that almost all of the children turned in the assignment, and that while she was grading them in class, a few students "made the comment that they thought this assignment was fun and they wanted to do more of them." She also reported that the activity was successful in making students "a lot more aware of differences between proper and common nouns."

Successes such as these prompted other teachers to try interactive homework assignments (project funding bought the TIPS series for all of the districts). A sixth-grade teacher posted a task that built on the idea of *waves* relating to real-life situations. Students interviewed their parents to determine whether living in a *high-risk* area would be worth the potential benefits. The idea of waves was introduced through the notion that waves in the form of earthquakes and volcanic activity are responsible for making an area high risk.

Overall interest from the group in the TIPS activities inspired an elementary school principal who participated in the project to write:

> As we make this a parent involvement activity and the children teach the songs they have learned to their parents, they enrich their families as well. I will visit each music classroom when the materials arrive, explain where the funding came from, and provide the students with a TIPS worksheet to take home and complete with their families. This home-school link will be a powerful way to build a broader understanding for our music program.

At the beginning of the project, faculty were concerned that teachers would struggle to create successful activities. As the project progressed, faculty encouraged teachers to work more toward the idea of interactive homework like TIPS to overcome many of the barriers they perceived initially.

Uses of Technology

Project funding paid for a limited number of resources for each district. Faculty members discussed with their participants ways that technology could enhance the home/school literacy tasks that they were developing. Many of the teachers decided to pool their funds to purchase shared resources, while others bought materials specific to their individual classroom contexts. Even simple technologies seemed to make a big difference in the home/school connections. Teachers commented on digital recorders and digital cameras, the Leapfrog electronic reading tools and other computer software, and take-home book/tape combinations. For example, one teacher demonstrated reading a book and then listening to the recording. The teacher reported that "the kids were so excited and eager to do it themselves." Each child chose a book that he or she could read independently and then read from the book into the recorder. The teacher writes:

> I wish I could have captured the expressions as they read their books and then listened to themselves. They did it over and over and giggled

and sparkled the whole time. Then they got creative and started telling their own stories with expression and sound effects. It was an hour of enthusiastic reading.

Similar enthusiasm was expressed for the use of digital cameras as a way of communicating with parents. One teacher sent students home with photos of class activities on the digital camera for parent feedback/response. Another teacher asked the students to take pictures of their immediate family members. The parents helped the children write brief summaries of the people in the family including information about the origin of their names. In addition, she asked the children to photograph special objects at home. The parents helped their children understand why the objects have special value or meaning. The overall purpose was to assemble a collection of photographs and short writings that created a picture of a family's unique identity. The teacher suggested taking close-up digital photos of valuable family pictures, thus avoiding any risk to irreplaceable family photos and albums.

Reasons for Success

The teachers reflected on why some tasks met with success and others failed. Teachers attributed some of the success to the encouragement of faculty and peers. Another reason appeared to be the implementation of the principles of interactive homework. For example, one teacher surmised that the TIPS activities were successful because the children were excited about the assignment in the first place, and they had the opportunity to share new learning and engaging activities with parents or family partners. She concluded that "parents were impressed with the technology" but at the same time successful home/school connection activities were "short, simple and meaningful."

Other reasons for success were also presented. One teacher noted that she always sent home a parent tip or strategy that the parents felt were helpful and made working with their children more enjoyable. Another teacher noted how useful TIPS were to her. In the activity on hairstyles, she noted that students liked the assignment and had a lot of questions regarding hairstyles of the past. She also commented that the students "seemed pretty giggly" when they turned in their assignments and described some of the hairstyles that were told to them. She concluded that "the TIPS activities were a life saver" for her, continuing that she "found the activities to be worthwhile and they brought the parents and students together." Other teachers commented that watching the children get excited about working with their parents made the teachers even more determined to understand how to make and keep these connections.

The most successful activities seemed to be the ones that followed the interactive homework guidelines but also had as content a way for parents to share their lives, interests, and values with their children. The response rates were higher and the students seemed more excited and engaged when the tasks included questions around topics such as how the parents learned to read or what the place was like where parents had lived as children. Comments indicated that success also arose from the teachers' willingness to work for/with their students and parents until they "got it right." By the end of the project, teachers' excitement over interactive homework that involved some kind of family connection was palpable, as illustrated in the following:

> I had an incredible conference week! All three of my Russian mothers came with a change in attitude. I shared with them that our school is doing a multi-cultural fair in May and that their child will be researching, reporting, and sharing an artifact of his/her country. They were very receptive and seemed excited about what their child could bring to school to share. Luba, one of my students, is bringing mom's samovar (a decorative tea pot) as her artifact. I was deeply touched by Luba's mom who, the day after her conference, sent me a gift ... a snow globe of Lenin's tomb. It seemed to be a gesture of friendship. I finally felt as though we had connected and she realized that we both had Luba's best interest in mind when it comes to school and her education. Making connections is really working and my students will be the better for it!

Teacher Changes and the Future

In the post survey of teachers, participating teachers were asked how involvement in this project had changed their ideas or behaviors. Half of the teachers (including the principals) responded to the follow-up survey. Overall, participants felt that the ideas that they were exposed to and allowed to work with had changed the communication between parents and teachers. Three related themes emerged from the follow-up survey: accountability, sensitivity, and enthusiasm. To begin with, teachers observed more accountability from students to complete assignments because parents were involved and interested. As one teacher noted:

> Assignment completion for my three trimester writing projects was over 90%—largely due to communication using computer based technology, due to deliberately making assignment choices that involved parents ... I believe that communication is much better now with [reading and writing]. The parents are actually seeing and working with them on the subjects due to the various activities. Also, with the comments section on the bottom [of the TIPS activities] the parents are keeping me informed of the needs of the child. [These activities made students] more responsible to communicate with their parents and work alongside with their parents.

Likewise, parents saw that their children's teachers had also become more accountable. By actively soliciting comments and feedback from parents through the interactive homework, teachers demonstrated their willingness to take into consideration the wishes of their students' parents.

Greater sensitivity is a second theme that emerged from the follow-up survey data. Teachers noted that through this project they felt more sensitive, understanding, and responsive to the different cultures in their school. They commented on issues of poverty and being more sensitive to this as well. The success of the interactive homework activities centered on their brevity and meaningfulness. Time with children was at a premium for many of the working parents in this project. Rather than excusing this simple fact, or worse yet, blaming parents, teachers chose to assign home/school activities that acknowledged the reality of work and family and attempted to structure time within this context. Whereas previously teachers had had very little communication with parents, suddenly two-way communication was vibrant and meaningful. Teachers noted a much higher level of communication with parents and began to see home-school connections as a regular and important part of every lesson. The change was felt at meetings with parents, where one teacher noted:

> We have gotten way more parents to our group meetings. Most of it was due to the impetus of this project. We also went into the presentations very, very confident because we had artifacts and work to share with the parents. That made the night qualitatively different from other parent meetings in the past. We were quite proud.

The third theme to emerge from the follow-up surveys was an overall greater level of enthusiasm from students for school. Teachers noted that the students who had previously not turned in assignments had, in the words of one teacher, "turned themselves around and are turning in assignments and in general reading a lot more. One student in particular is so eager to learn and is turning in his assignments. He will even stay in during recess to complete his assignments!" Not surprisingly, when students are excited about their assignments, parents tend to be more excited to work with their children and continue the learning at home. As one teacher initially commented: "so much of our school day ends at the bell. The kids seem loathe to do any school work at home." She later explained that the digital voice recorders and interactive homework activities seemed to have broken that cycle, and in turn, she too felt more enthusiastic.

Teachers and principals indicated their continuing desire to connect with parents in the future. One teacher mentioned starting the interactive (TIPS) activities earlier in the year in order to "start the year off on the right foot" and maintaining communication with parents at regular intervals—not just during conferences. Other teachers who noticed that parent involvement positively influenced student attitude toward homework plan to incorporate parents in additional activities. Many teachers commented on the value of technology and feedback from parents. A principal who participated in the project planned to encourage other teachers in the school to adopt similar techniques and technologies. Thus, the follow-up surveys from teachers indicated clear long-term goals to continue implementing what they learned through their participation in the project.

Conclusions

One teacher summed up the outcomes of this project for the teachers and the students:

> The project got me out of complacency mode and into action mode. It gave me a target and a purpose. The kids responded so much more enthusiastically than I ever thought they would ... On Saturday nights as they are cruising in their cars they are listening to CDs of their plays and stories that we have recorded. I thought that was pretty cool.

Two of our project goals were to help teachers involve parents in the literacy achievement of their children and to develop responsible, effective, technologically enhanced partnerships between teachers and parents. Although barriers to home/school connections still exist for these teachers, this project supported them in exploring how to facilitate literacy through home/school tasks and to make connections with parents that can help students achieve. Participants did not have to create parent interest or to invent new activities—teachers merely gave parents and families the opportunity to engage in a timely way with their children in meaningful, achievable tasks that they developed for their specific content and contexts. The interest from the families existed, but through interactive homework they were provided a vehicle that had previously not existed to demonstrate that interest. The increase in returned homework assignments that the teachers noted suggests that more students were accessing the content and language of the lesson; although not measured here, this indicates that students may have greater achievement in those areas.

Another goal was to provide a model for professional development in home/school literacy connections. This experience confirms that situated learning can form a strong basis for teacher educators to engage in successful professional development in home/school literacy connections. The outcomes of this project emphasize the importance of basing professional development experiences for teachers on research on how teachers learn. By employing a situated learning framework in which teachers could work within their own curriculum with their own students and community, this project helped teachers reflect on and develop appropriate home-school interactions. Equally important was connecting the teachers, as Herrington and Oliver (2000) suggest, to others who served as peers and experts and provided ongoing mentoring. In addition, providing teachers with a strong and clear emphasis for their professional development, in this case scaffolded reading experiences, helped teachers to focus on an attainable challenge. We recommend that teachers and administrators look for these components when considering professional development experiences and that teacher educators consider these points when developing professional development.

We also recommend to university faculty that they participate as colleagues in situated experiences with teachers. Through collaboration with our teacher-participants, we shared and reinforced our understandings about home/school interactions. Although these insights are expressed in the literature on teaching, they did not seem real until they became lived experiences for the participants. Together we learned how to structure assignments most fruitfully; to give parents and students as many clear guidelines as possible; to keep tasks simple and focused; and to consider parents' and students' interests and connections to the materials. We concluded that interactive homework assignments were useful, effective, and relatively simple tasks for school to home literacy connections for parents with diverse backgrounds. As important, we underscored the need for teachers to have time and support to work together and resources that allow participants to continue to develop parent connections, as they have expressed the desire to do. This model of ongoing participation and facilitation in situated contexts, then, proved effective for faculty, teachers, parents, and students.

Some of these ideas are relatively new, while others have been suggested in the literature but not necessarily implemented during professional development experiences. However, integrating them into effective, ongoing professional development within teacher classrooms can help more teachers out of complacency and into action.

Appendix A: Resources for Communication With Parents

Au, K.H., & Mason, J.M. (1981). Social organization factors in learning to read: The balance of rights hypothesis. *Reading Research Quarterly*, *17*(1), 115–152.

A report of a key case study in which two Hawaiian classrooms were compared. Demonstrated that when there is a difference between interactions around print between home and school, teachers who incorporate home interaction patterns in their classrooms bring about more effective learning.

Auerbach, E. (1995). Deconstructing the discourse of strengths in family literacy. *Journal of Reading Behavior*, *27*(4), 643–661.

Describes different approaches that have been taken with family literacy programs including a historically prevalent "deficit" model in which it is assumed that parents have little to offer and homes need to be remedied. Points to a better direction: valuing and incorporating the literacies that children bring with them to the classroom.

Davern, L. (2004). School-to-home notebooks. *Teaching Exceptional Children*, *36*(5), 22–27.

Describes reasons that teachers have turned to notebooks as ways to communicate with parents. Includes questions to consider in the use of the notebooks. Reports on informal research of parents' responses to the notebook use.

Dyson, L.L. (2001). Home-school communication and expectations of recent Chinese immigrants. *Canadian Journal of Education*, *26*(3), 455–476.

Reports interview research with Chinese immigrant families regarding home-school communication with the findings that communication rarely occurred between parents and teachers, the communication occurred for different reasons and through different means than that carried out by nonimmigrant families. The parents desired a more detailed description of their children's academic work.

Goldenberg, C., Reese, L., & Gallimore, R. (1992). Effects of literacy materials from school on Latino children's home experiences and early reading achievement. *American Journal of Education*, *100*(4), 497–536.

Reports research on the impact of two types of home-learning materials on Spanish-speaking kindergarteners from Mexico and Central America: books to be read for enjoyment and phonics activities to work on discrete sound-grapheme relationships. The parents did not use the storybooks as the teachers had intended, choosing to focus on the correcting their children's sound-grapheme production. Points to the idea that parents need better communication about teachers' expectations about literacy interactions.

Heath, S.B. (1983). *Ways with words*. Cambridge: Cambridge University Press.

A book that describes qualitative research in two communities in the Southern United States regarding home literacy activities. The communities were comprised of a lower-class African-American community and a middle-class White community. Children encountered rich literacy activities at home in both communities, but only the interactions in the middle-class homes closely resembled the literacy interaction patterns found in classrooms. Suggests that teachers need to be aware of home literacy practices and bridge home and school for students to increase learning.

Jimenez, R.T. (2000). Literacy and the identity development of Latina/o students. *American Educational Research Journal, 37*(4), 971–1000.

Reports research with 9–12-year-old native Spanish-speaking students in regards to their identities as both English and Spanish users. Includes information about how children make their way between two worlds, how their parents interact with them around literacy, and the role of literacy activities such as letter writing in their lives.

Johnson, C.E., & Viramontez, R.P. (2004). Latino parents in the rural Southeast: A study of family and school partnerships. *Journal of Family and Consumer Sciences, 96*(4), 29–33.

Briefly reports on interview research with teachers and Latino parents in a school district about the quality of communication that occurred between homes and schools. The report gives insight into the challenges and strengths that both groups perceived to exist in the district.

Li, G. (2001). Family literacy and cultural identity: An ethnographic study of a Filipino family in Canada. *McGill Journal of Education, 35*(1), 9–29.

Reports on qualitative research of one Filipino immigrant family, giving insight into the literacy activities of the individuals in the family as well as the literacy activities that they all shared. Demonstrates the extreme importance of shared family identity through these literacy activities.

Li, G. (2004). Perspectives on struggling English language learners: Case studies of two Chinese-Canadian children. *Journal of Literacy Research, 36*(1), 31–72.

Reports on a qualitative study of two native Chinese-speakers in a Grade 4/5 classroom and in their homes. Findings suggest that a lack of a bridge between home and school cultures was largely responsible for the difficulties that the students experienced with literacy.

Noll, E. (1998). Experiencing literacy in and out of school: Case studies of two American Indian youths. *Journal of Literacy Research, 30*(2), 205–232.

A report on a case study of two teenage students—one Dakota and one Lakota—regarding how they used literacy in school and at home. They used reading and writing as a means to understand and participate in culture as well as create their identities. The findings suggest that cultural literacy patterns "run deep," and teachers need to actively investigate them.

Salend, S.J., Duhaney, D., Anderson, D.J., & Gottschalk, C. (2004). Using the internet to improve homework communication and completion. *Teaching Exceptional Children*, *36*(3), 64–73.

   Describes the option of using a website to facilitate communication between parents and teachers about homework. Contains suggestions for effective use.

Villas-Boas, A. (1998). The effects of parental involvement in homework on student achievement in Portugal and Luxembourg. *Childhood Education*, *74*(6), 367–371.

   Report on research in European schools in which a correlation was suggested between parent homework orientation meetings and students' completion rate of homework.

Volk, D. (1994). A case study of parent involvement in the homes of three Puerto Rican kindergarteners. *The Journal of Educational Issues of Language Minority Students*, *14*(1), 89–114.

   Reports case study research of three economically poor Puerto Rican kindergarteners regarding the types of interactions that parents carried out with the children around literacy activities. All the parents were involved in the children's lives with literacy, but this involvement varied in terms of the parents' communication patterns, including how much "teacher-talk" was used and the language(s) chosen for the communication.

Weigel, D.J., Martin, S.S., & Bennett, K.K. (2005). Ecological influences of the home and the child-care center on preschool-age children's literacy development. *Reading Research Quarterly*, *40*(2), 204–233.

   Quantitative survey research of adults in preschoolers' lives regarding literacy activities and knowledge. Findings include the idea that all adults across children's lives who engage children in activities around print had an impact on children's literacy knowledge.

Appendix B: Questionnaire for Teachers

A slightly adapted version of this survey was given to parents and students.

Instructions

Please answer the questions as specifically but concisely as possible. Your answers will help us to understand your needs as we work together.

1. In the past, how has successful communication occurred with your students' parents?
2. What are your goals in communicating with your students' parents?
3. How would you characterize the ideal communication with your students' parents?
4. What role do you think technology could take in meeting this ideal communication between parents and teachers?
5. How would you characterize communication with parents regarding your child's progress in reading and writing?
6. What do you believe good reading progress looks like?
7. Do you believe parents are doing an adequate job in making sure this progress occurs? Why or why not?
8. What are your beliefs about what helps a student make reading progress?
9. What are the roles of parents and what are the roles of teachers in promoting the reading progress that children make?
10. What are your expectations of the role that you will take with your students outside of class time? How available do you believe teachers should be after the school day ends and in the summer?
11. From what you know so far about this grant project (Partners), what are your expectations? What do you hope to accomplish by the end of the project?

References

Andersen, J., Reder, L. and Simon, H. (1996) Situated learning and education. *Educational Researcher* **25**:(4), pp. 5–11.

August, D. and Shanahan, T. (eds) (2006) *Developing literacy in second-language learners: Report of the national literacy panel on language-minority children and youth*. Routledge (LEA), New York.

Beck, I. L., McKeown, M. G., Sinatra, G. M. and Loxterman, U. J. A. (1991) Revising social studies text from a text-processing perspective: Evidence of improved comprehensibility. *Reading Research Quarterly* **26**, pp. 251–276.

Bogdan, R. and Biklen, S. (2003) *Qualitative research for education: An introduction to theories and methods* (4th ed), Allyn & Bacon/Pearson, Boston, MA.

Brown, J., Collins, A. and Duguid, P. (1989) Situated cognition and the culture of learning. *Educational Researcher* **18**:(1), pp. 32–42.

Creswell, J. (2003) *Research design: Qualitative, quantitative, and mixed method approaches* (2nd ed.), Sage, Thousand Oaks, CA

Droop, M. and Verhoeven, L. (1998) Background knowledge, linguistic complexity, and second-language reading comprehension. *Journal of Literacy Research* **30**, pp. 253–271

Englert, C. S., Tarrant, K. L., Mariage, T. V. and Oxer, T. (1994) Lesson talk as the work of reading groups: The effectiveness of two interventions. *Journal of Reading Disabilities* **27**:(3), pp. 165–185.

Epstein, J. (1996) School-family-community partnerships: Caring for the children we share. *Phi Delta Kappan* **76**, pp. 701–712.

Epstein, J., Sanders, M., Simon, B., Salinas, K., Jansorn, N. and Van Voorhis, F. (2002) *School, family, and community partnerships: Your handbook for action* (2nd ed.), Corwin Press, Thousand Oaks, CA — Retrieved October 16, 2008, from http://www.csos.jhu.edu/P2000/tips/index.htm

Epstein, J., Simon, B. and Salinas, K. (1997) Involving parents in homework in the middle grades. *Phi Delta Kappa Research Bulletin* **18.**

Epstein, J. and Van Voorhis, F. (2001) More than minutes: Teachers' roles in designing homework. *Educational Psychologist* **36**, pp. 181–194.

Feiman-Nemser, S., Remillard, J. and Murray, F. B. (ed) (1996) Perspectives on learning to teach. *The teacher educator's handbook: Building a knowledge base for the preparation of teachers* pp. 63–91. Jossey-Bass, San Francisco — Retrieved April 24, 2008, from http://ncrtl.msu.edu/http/ipapers/html/ip953.htm

Fisher, U. (1994) Learning word from context and dictionaries: An experimental comparison. *Applied Psycholinguistics* **15**, pp. 551–574.

Fitzgerald, J. and Graves, M. F. (2004) *Scaffolding reading experiences for English-language learners.* Christopher-Gordon, Norwood, MA.

Griffin, M. (1995) You can't get there from here: Situated learning, transfer, and map skills. *Contemporary Educational Psychology* **20**, pp. 65–87.

Hendricks, C. (2001) Teaching causal reasoning through cognitive apprenticeship: What are results from situated learning? *Journal of Educational Research* **94**:(5), pp. 302–311.

Herrington, J. and Oliver, R. (2000) An instructional design framework for authentic learning environments. *Educational Technology Research and Development* **48**:(3), pp. 23–48.

Kennedy, M., Raths, J. D. and McAninch, A. C. (eds) (1999) Ed schools and the problem of knowledge. *Advances in teacher education volume 5: What counts as knowledge in teacher education?* pp. 29–45. Ablex , Stamford, CT.

Lave, J. and Wenger, E. (1991) *Situated learning: Legitimate peripheral participation* Cambridge University Press, Cambridge.

L'Engle, M. (1973, reissue) *Wrinkle in time.* Yearling Books, New York.

McMeniman, M. and Evans, R. (1998) CALL through the eyes of teachers and learners of Asian languages: Panacea or business as usual? *On-CALL Online* **12**:(1)

Nathenson-Mejia, S. (1994) Bridges between home and school: Literacy building activities for non-English speaking homes. *Journal of Educational Issues of Language Minority Students* **14**, pp. 149–164.

National Center for Research on Teacher Learning (NCRTL) (1994) *Findings on learning to teach* Michigan State University, East Lansing, MI — Retrieved April 24, 2008, from http://ncrtl.msu.edu/http/folt.pdf

Palincsar, A. S. and Brown, A. L. (1984) Reciprocal teaching of comprehension—fostering and monitoring activities. *Cognition and Instruction* **1**, pp. 117–175.

Putnam, R. and Borko, H. (2000) What do new views of knowledge and thinking have to say about research on teacher learning? *Educational Researcher* **29**:(1), pp. 4–15

Rudney, G. (2005) *Every teacher's guide to working with parents.* Corwin Press, Thousand Oaks, CA.

Schon, D. (1987) *Educating the reflective practitioner.* Jossey-Bass, San Francisco.

Shulman, L. (1987) Knowledge and teaching: Foundation of the new reform. *Harvard Educational Review* **57**, pp. 1–22.

Valdes, G. (1996) *Con respeto: Bridging distances between culturally diverse families and schools.* Teachers College Press, New York.

Van Voorhis, F. (2001) Interactive science homework: An experiment in home and school connections. *NASSP Bulletin* **85**, pp. 20–32.

ARTICLE 2: READING GIRLS: LIVING LITERATE AND POWERFUL LIVES

Authors: Pam Bettis, Mary F. Roe
Affiliation: Washington State University, Pullman, WA

Abstract

In this qualitative study, the authors merge two bodies of previously separated scholarship: (1) a socio-cultural understanding of adolescent girls in light of the shifting meaning of ideal girlhood, and (2) the participation and success of adolescent girls in school-based literacy activities. They apply these fields of inquiry to explore the following questions: (1) What does it mean to be a young woman/girl in middle school? (2) What does it mean to be a young woman/girl reader in middle school? (3) What does it mean to be a young woman/girl in literacy circles and discussion groups? To answer these questions, the authors collected observational and interview data in two classrooms (one grade 6 and one grade 8) from January to June. From the analysis of the data, the authors identify profiles that typify the girls with whom they interacted, capture the girls' roles during literature discussion groups and other classroom events, and frame the influence of teachers' actions on the girls.

Introduction

Girls. Reading. Reading girls. Girl power. Instead of posing these ideas as having defined boundaries and unique ideas linked to them, we think they warrant a consolidated consideration. Therefore, we conducted a qualitative study that merges these two bodies of previously separated scholarship:

(1) a socio-cultural understanding of adolescent girls in light of the shifting meaning of ideal girlhood,
(2) the participation and success of adolescent girls in school-based literacy activities.

Often the first body of literature remains theoretically focused (Inness, 1998; Walkerdine, 1990), and when it is empirically applied, the focus is often on popular culture (e.g., Inness, 1999), extracurricular activities (Adams & Bettis, 2003), or a more general understanding of female identity in school (Brown & Gilligan, 1992; Orenstein, 1994). Specific academic practices are rarely considered.

Recently, best-selling author and Harvard psychologist, Dan Kindlon, considered the current status of girls in *Alpha girls: Understanding the new American girl and how she is changing the world* (2006), and argued that a new psychology of girls (i.e., a psychology of emancipation) has produced a girl very different from the girl in crisis who dominated the media in the early 1990s. This alpha girl is poised to change the world, economically, politically, and socially. Kindlon viewed this new girl as a hybrid, one who embodies the best traits of masculinity and femininity. Thus, she is confident, assertive, competitive, autonomous, future oriented, risk taking, as well as collaborative, relationship oriented, and not obsessed with boyfriends or her physical appearance.

Kindlon's (2006) tone is celebratory and quite a contrast to the manner in which girls have been portrayed in past years in both popular and scholarly works. During the past 15 years, girls have been alternately framed as passive, without voice, sassy, slutty, and mean. What do these changing discourses of girlhood mean to girls? How might these changing discourses of girlhood play out in their school practices? How might female teachers understand their work in light of these discourses? This leads to the second body of relevant scholarship.

Those scholars who consider adolescent girls' literacy activities often neglect the discursive practices of ideal girlhood and investigate girls' literacy practices as if they exist in a gender-blind vacuum. When literacy scholars do consider gender, the lines of inquiry take several turns. Some note the gendered predispositions held by boys and girls toward reading (Appleman, 2006). For example, Smith and Wilhelm (2002) unveiled the practical way that many young men look at things they do. For these boys, and as the title of this work suggests, "reading don't fix no Chevys" and therefore reading holds less value in their lives. Girls lean toward "real stuff." For them, this includes attention to their emotional and lived experiences (Smith, 2000). Other scholars consider in and out of school reading (e.g., Hull & Schultz, 2002). Some scholars explore gendered discursive practices (Alvermann, Commeyras, Young, Randall, & Hinson, 1997), while others consider whether a classroom culture might influence patterns of gendered behaviors (e.g., Hinchman, Payne-Bourcy, Thomas, & Olcott, 2002). Though the influence of class (i.e., a student's economic position in the wider community) often finds inclusion in a broader and cultural consideration of literacy practices (e.g., Jones, 2006), directly considering the influence of girls' concepts of themselves on their accomplishments as readers in public middle schools forges new ground.

As many scholars of girlhood have documented (Adams 1999; Bettis & Adams, 2005; Budgeon, 1998; Harris, 2004a, 2004b; Hunter, 2002; Inness, 1998; McRobbie, 1993; Mitchell, 1995; Nelson & Vallone, 1994; Walkerdine, 1993), ideal girlhood is constantly being rewritten. The early 1990s concern for our "girl poisoning culture" (Pipher, 1994) and the worrisome research published by the American Association for University Women (AAUW, 1992; 1998) positioned girls as passive victims, ones who lost their voice during adolescence. However, at the end of the century, a Girl Power movement, embraced by both girls and corporate America, positioned girls as smart, sassy, assertive, and independent (Bettis & Adams, 2005; Harris, 2004a, 2004b). Feminist scholars have argued that new subject positions are being made available to girls that provide a counter discourse to the girl as passive victim.

Our qualitative study builds on these ideas by exploring how girls in grades 6 and 8 define themselves as young women, particularly in relation to their understandings of "ideal girlhood." Then, the project turns to how these adolescent girls define themselves as young readers. Here, the goal is to understand how the cultural model girls present for themselves in their personal lives apprentices (Lave & Wenger, 1991) them for membership in classroom literacy experiences. The following questions initially guided this study: (1) What does it mean to be a young woman/girl in middle school? (2) What does it mean to be a young woman/girl reader in middle school? (3) What does it mean to be a young woman/ girl in literacy circles and discussion groups?

Theoretical Framework

For this inquiry, we employ the theoretical tools of both critical feminism and feminist post structuralism to help us understand this contradictory space of girlhood and how girls live their lives in classrooms and as readers. Drawing from a rich body of critical feminist research (e.g., Devault, 1996; Fine & Weis, 1998; Marshall, 1997, 1999), we nestle our study at the juncture of cultural and structural explanations for life in school. Critical feminism reminds us of how race, ethnicity, and particularly social class in our study are markers of power and privilege. Further, critical feminism keeps us focused on the everyday experiences and material realities of the girls we observed (Devault, 1996; Lather, 1991).

Following Davies (1989, 1993, 1999), Walkerdine (1990), Kenway and Willis (1998), and Harris (2004a, 2004b), we also employ feminist poststructuralism as a theoretical tool for examining how girls make sense of their own identities as girls and as readers amidst a changing gender landscape. Feminist poststructuralism encouraged us to explore how girls described ideal girlhood and how they negotiated the traditionally feminine marker of "nice." We argue that both of these discourses, that of ideal girlhood and nice, play a part in how girls see themselves as readers and how they participate in reading within and outside of the classroom. Feminist poststructuralism does not position girls as passive beings but rather as persons located within history, produced in a do-it-yourself philosophy, and practiced in that philosophy. We move these understandings forward to the roles of middle school girls in their language arts classrooms.

Literatures Reviewed

The claim that today's girls are living a "psychology of emancipation" is an optimistic one, especially when juxtaposed to the claims made about girls over the last 15 years. During the early 1990s, the image of girls was one of passive and voiceless victims who suffered in a girl poisoning culture. According to Mary Pipher, author of the 1994 best seller *Reviving Ophelia*, girls' potential was swallowed in a Bermuda Trianglesque society. Research findings from the American Association of University Women on the status of girls along with other popular books such as *Schoolgirls* (Orenstein, 1994) and *Between Voice and Silence* (Taylor, Gilligan, & Sullivan, 1995) led to a plethora of organizations, activities (i.e., Take Our Daughters to Work Day), and curriculum changes that would address the needs of girls. Scholars who looked at girls' literacy also acted on a need to move from studying literacy as a psychological process to a social practice. Within this cultural and social perspective, gender mattered. For example, Barbieri (1995) came to see her view that "they [her students] were individuals more than they were boys or girls ... did them a disservice" (p. 7). She chronicled her interactions with a group of seventh grade girls during a period when she served as their English teacher. She sought to empower these girls to read, write, and simultaneously consider questions of personal importance. These girls, whom Barbieri acknowledged as "privileged," attended an all-girl private school. Barbieri learned quickly that they, in spite of their educational advantages, sacrificed their authentic opinions and feelings in their quest to be an "ideal" girl. Barbieri's belief that "it's the girls who are in the greatest danger of slipping away from us, quietly, unobtrusively, politely slipping away" (p. xi) fueled her quest to offer a curriculum that did better by them as well as to document and report her findings. In the same vein, Cherland (1994) broadened a look at literacy to include a cultural context. She studied seven sixth-grade girls' reading of fiction in and out of school. In her view, gender is a cultural construction and reading, as a social practice, unavoidably involves gender. For these girls, their gender made it acceptable to read and acknowledge the importance of reading to their lives. Their reading of fiction also allowed them to fulfill the social expectations placed upon them. For example, being a friend accompanied being a girl. These girls linked this responsibility by reading books in common, conversing with other girls about the books they read, and lending books to other girls.

By the late 1990s, the girl as victim image had given way to sassy, girly girls with can do attitudes. The Girl Power movement, whose origins emerged from a combination of punk rock music and accompanying alternative lifestyle along with feminist sensibilities, heralded a new type of girl—one who celebrated her femininity and, at the same time, practiced a do-it-yourself philosophy. This new sensibility paralleled increases in girls' participation in sports, popular music, and violent crimes, and their increasing economic influence. Not surprisingly, the Girl Power movement was quickly commodified. Laura Croft, Xena, the Spice Girls, and cartoon superheroes, the Power Puffs, were all seen as a symbolic shift from passive girl to empowered girl.

By the turn of the century, that empowerment had become somewhat problematic. Social critics pointed to girls' promiscuity and "relational aggression" or meanness, particularly toward other girls, as evidence of girls losing the traditional markers of femininity. The popularity of the movies *Mean Girls* and *13* along with the best-selling books, *Queen Bees and Wannabees* and *Sluts*, spoke to these concerns. With Kindlon's (2006) new book, *Alpha Girls*, once again a shift occurred in the landscape of girlhood. Kindlon attributed the emergence of this group of girls to several factors. First, the fruits of the second wave of feminism such as a decrease in stereotypical female media images, the large number of girls who play competitive sports (thanks to Title IX), and the role models of women who have pursued a variety of challenging careers have contributed to the psychology of alpha girls. For Kindlon, the important roles that fathers have taken on in the rearing of children have been significant. In their increased involvement with their children, particularly their daughters, fathers have introduced girls to "male ways of being." These masculine dispositions have been passed on to daughters through fathers' involvement in sports and the sharing of their hobbies and interests. Alpha girls have adopted these masculine skills and dispositions. When these internal changes are combined with a changed social context produced by the women's movement, the new hybrid alpha girl emerges. Although Kindlon noted that a majority of his data was collected from affluent White girls, he still maintains, "alpha girl psychology … transcends barriers of race and class" (p. xvii). In his view, all girls at the turn of this century and regardless of their race, social class, sexual orientation, geographical location, religious affiliation, or physical capabilities, differ from their female predecessors because they have choices.

The theme of choice is prevalent throughout Kindlon's arguments and much of the Girl Power discourse. Some girls may still suffer from bulimia, depression, and low self-esteem, but generally, girls are the new winners of a drastically changed cultural and social context that offers them unlimited choices. "Girls today have more choices about how to act, who to be, and what is considered 'normal,' culturally sanctioned behavior. This is precisely what their mothers and grandmothers fought for—the ability and freedom to *choose* how to live one's live" (Kindlon, 2006, p. 28, emphasis original).

Investigations of girls' literate lives have also moved forward with more direct consideration of literary and feminist theory. Blackford (2004) interviewed 33 girls from various geographical locations and ethnic backgrounds. She unveiled the importance of aesthetic reading for these girls and its role in expanding their personal and worldviews. However, her work falls short of going into the classroom to understand better the current overlays between girls' sense of themselves as readers in and out of school.

Thus, over the past 20 years, girls have been framed and reframed from passive victims with low self-esteem to Kindlon's (2006) proposed alpha girls who can solve society's political, social, and economic problems. The role of gender in their reading has moved from the background to take a central role. Popular discourses have consequences in how society thinks about and solves social problems and how individual girls make sense of their lives, intellectually and emotionally. However, academics whose work focuses on gendered literacy rarely consider the influence of such popular girlhood discourses on the schooling process and the school discourse of literacy learning.

Finally, the body of information about literacy and young

adolescents (e.g., Irvin & Rycik, 2001; Roe, 2004) and, more specifically, the various forms of literature discussion groups contribute in
an important way to this project. We limit these comments to literature discussion groups.

The option for reader response to literature takes roots from the
work of scholars such as Rosenblatt (1978) and Langer (1995) and
shifts reading instruction away from scripted lessons to opportunities for text engagement and exploration. In addition, it moves these
explorations from the typical teacher posed questions and student
response "discussions" to small group, student-centered exchanges
(e.g., Almasi, 1995; Daniels, 1994; Eeds & Wells, 1989; Goatley, Brock,
& Raphael, 1995). Across the various versions of literature discussion groups such as Book Club and Literature Circles, basic features
emerge: (a) book selection by students, (b) organization of small
groups, (c) and discussions intended to foster an enriched grasp of
the selected text (Gunning, 2004). These features provide rich opportunities for students, and especially girls, to exert their independence
and thought. Interestingly, however, once these scholars characterized
the parameters and benefits of literature discussion groups, research
has remained silent on their everyday use by typical teachers and students. Therefore, in this study, we address that vacuum between girls'
portrayal of themselves and girls' roles as readers in those classrooms
that feature a form of literature discussion groups.

Method

We determined that a qualitative design best suited our intention to
understand the potential overlaps and digressions between adolescents' female identity and their literacy practices (e.g., Denzin & Lincoln, 2005). First, it captures a way to explore our overall curiosity
about student descriptions of themselves and their participation in
their language arts classes. As Marshall and Rossman (1989) stated,
"in qualitative research, questions and problems for research most often come from real-world observations, dilemmas, and questions" (p.
28). Second, qualitative method provides direction for analyzing the
types of information this classroom-based project generated: observations, interviews, and documents. Third, it embraces situated learning

environments as a benefit to cultural understanding rather than an interference to it (Schratz, 1993). Finally, qualitative method coincides with our emic stance. As Gall, Gall, and Borg (2005) explained, this involves obtaining "the research participants' perceptions and understanding of their social reality" (p. 548).

Context

We conducted this research in a middle school located in a university town of 26,000 residents in the northwest. The community members whose children attended the school represented a mix of wheat farmers, university faculty, graduate students, blue-collar workers, and white-collar employees. While small and rural in location, the town's diverse community allowed diversity within its student population. Specifically, the school district reported its racial/ethnic demographics as 76% White; 11% Asian/Pacific Islander; 7% Hispanic; 4% Black; and 2% American Indian. Of importance, two teachers in this school, a sixth grade language arts and an eighth grade language arts/social studies teacher, reported their use of literature discussion groups—the literacy event that we intended to target. After meeting with them to explain the goal of our investigation and its features, they willingly agreed to offer their classrooms as our research sites.

Data Sources

To answer our research questions, we acquired data from four sources typical of qualitative analysis: (1) classroom observations, (2) documents, i.e., assignment explanations, scoring rubrics for class assignments, and in-class worksheets, (3) 47 student interviews, and (4) two teacher interviews. To establish continuity and build familiarity with the participants and their classroom context, the first author observed and interviewed in the eighth grade sections and the second author collected data for the sixth grade. Next, we explain the particulars of our collection of these data.

Observations. Our observation period extended from January to June. We attended two sections of each teacher's regularly scheduled language arts periods, a total of four language arts sections. We tried to observe each class section on the days that these teachers planned literature discussion activities. However, this event occurred less frequently than we anticipated. Therefore, we expanded our observations to capture girls' participation in classroom discussions as well as their typical behaviors during a class period. We continued these general and targeted observations until we no longer noted anything not captured in previous observations that related to our research questions. In the end, we tallied 78 observations across these four sections. We created files from the handwritten field notes generated from each observation and entered them into *Ethnograph* (Qaulis Research Associates, 1998), a qualitative data analysis program.

Interviews. We conducted semi-structured interviews toward the end of our classroom observations with students and teachers. The individually conducted and audiotaped student interviews included the girls who submitted a permission form signed by them and their parent or guardian. This resulted in interviews with all but four students in the sixth grade classes (N = 25) and 22 girls in eighth grade classes (12 from an honors section and 10 in the general track). During the interviews, we used prepared questions to explore the girls' perceptions of themselves as girls and as participants in literature discussion groups and other classroom events. In keeping with open-ended and qualitative interviews, we used follow up questions to explore their responses to our prepared questions and to expand upon ideas they mentioned that pertained to our research questions (see Appendix A).

We used informal conversations with each teacher to understand better a day's events and their responses to them. Toward the end of our observation period, we designed prepared questions to guide a more focused exploration of these teachers' perceptions of their female students' attributes and their participation in literature discussion groups and other classroom events (see Appendix B). Like the student interviews, we transcribed our recording of these interviews. Then, we entered all individual interview files into *Ethnograph* (Qualis Research Associates, 1998).

Documents. We collected documents that the students received during our observation period. They included explanations for class projects, activity sheets that students completed, expectations for the literature discussion groups, and scoring rubrics for various assignments. These documents contributed to our understanding of these teachers' planning as well as the students' expectations for completing planned lessons and activities.

Data Analysis

Our analysis of these data proceeded in stages. Once our data collection period ended, we used a subset of these observations and interviews for initial coding (e.g., Lancy, 1993; LeCompte, Millroy, & Preissle, 1992). Next, we compared our open coding schemes and, as appropriate, collapsed them. We met once again to settle on a final set of codes, which we applied in common to our observations and interviews. We again verified our consistent use of our codes. (See Appendix C for the final set of observation codes and Appendix D for the interview codes.) Finally, we created coded files in *Ethnograph* (Qualis Research Associates, 1988). We used this software program to aggregate individually coded segments across these data. At times, we counted instances of coded segments and used these frequency counts to make sense of the relative recurrences of certain behaviors or events. Ultimately, we collapsed information across these sources to understand our research questions.

Results: The Girls

Seventy-seven years ago, Virginia Wolfe argued that girls and women needed to have "a room of one's own" where they might find the solitude and privacy to read, think, and write. Since that time, many girls certainly have obtained rooms of their own, but the rooms appear empty. With the passage of Title IX and the Girl Empowerment Movement, many girls now live the new markers of ideal girlhood. For these girls, these markers include their participation in sports and community arts programs and their claims of self-assertiveness and self-confidence. In fact, many of the girls we interviewed demonstrated characteristics of alpha girls, and appeared to draw from both traditionally feminine as well as masculine ways of being.

For example, an eighth grade Honors student, Erica, participates in volleyball, basketball, track, and dance team, which require after-school practices. When asked about her reading practices, she commented, "I read magazines and stuff. I don't really read books as much. … If I read a long book then it takes me a long time and I just want to get to the end of the book." Martie, a sixth grader, voices a comparable concern. As she states, "I'm not like a big reader … I like to do sports and be active." Further, instead of being concerned about whether they were considered "nice," a traditional feminine marker, these girls critiqued the concept. As eighth grader Julian observes, "I think nice is overrated. Beth and Sarah, they're like super nice, but they're really boring … I want to brag about myself. I'm kind of vain." A sixth grader, Marissa, describes herself as "energetic and wild" and considers the term nice to be "kind of a soft word to me. And it seems like I wouldn't use that because I'm not soft."

However, our field notes revealed a more complex and at times contradictory living of normative girlhood in the classroom. Girls who set aside reading for dance or soccer would use extra class time to read. While eighth grade girls spoke out and answered questions in equal numbers to the boys and sixth grade girls dominated literature discussion groups and whole class discussions, these numerical observations were offset by examples of girls acquiescing to boys' supposed intellectual prowess and their support for gender stereotypes. For example, we observed Honors student and class officer Vivian in an eighth grade small group activity with two boys taking the role of secretary and describing the two boys as the "thinkers." Sixth grade Jennifer presented another example of contradictory behavior; while she would take control of a literature discussion group in order to meet the teacher's expectations, she would also leave the group to chat with other girls around the drinking fountain.

Overall, these girls lack a coherent wholeness between their explanations and actions. Their challenge reflects an observation in the adolescent novel, *Criss Cross* (Perkins, 2005): "And any one place can make you go forward, or backward, or neither, but gradually you find all your pieces, your important pieces, and they stay with you, so that you're your whole self no matter where you go" (p. 267). These girls, for now, remain divided between compliance and willfulness, personal activities and personal reading, social proclivities and educational attainment. We use a selection of their profiles to capture the complex interplay of their lives and better pinpoint the import for powerful girls and readers.

Eighth Grade Girls

Kat: Alpha girl. Kat sits at a crowded cafeteria table, which is surrounded by girls who cannot find a seat. Laughter and chatter abound and Kat is in the center of most it. She is an Honors student who is well known by her classmates as well as other students outside the Honors enclave and was elected class vice president at the end of her eighth grade year. She is a tall and slender Chinese American adolescent who consistently wears faded blue jeans with a cotton belt that frequently misses one loop and a tee shirt.

In many ways, Kat exemplifies the new alpha girl. She is consistently mentioned by the other Honors students as someone they admire because she is willing to enter the fray of their class discussions. She is an athlete, musician, snowboarder, Honors student, and class officer and is not as concerned about her physical presentation as many other girls are.

When asked to describe herself, she and another Honors female student, state that they are talkative, friendly, active, and smart. A reader is not included in this initial list of descriptors. However, when asked to describe the ideal girl of today, Kat turns to a book read in sixth grade, *Stargirl* (Spinelli, 2000), and uses the central character to explain the ideal girl of today. "It was this book that we read in sixth grade. It's this girl who's not really pretty or anything. But she's like original. But she's not perfect. She's not like everyone else. She goes out into the desert and she meditates. She's very cool."

Like many of the girls involved in athletics, Kat does not necessarily perceive herself an athlete. Many girls saw themselves as participants in athletics and as physically active but not as athletes. Both Kat and her fellow interviewee, Val, describe themselves as active although both play soccer. Kat adds that she is a snowboarder and a hiker and

Val mentions that she likes to ski. The individualism, competitiveness, and aggressiveness that are supposedly learned during the practice of athletics are not apparent in how Kat describes her role as a soccer team member. In fact, she claims, "my thing about soccer is having friends."

This relationship orientation regarding her sports participation is also central to her understanding of herself as a major classroom discussion participant, one admired by others for offering her ideas. When asked what she liked about herself when she participated in class discussions, Kat responded, "I just like when people agree with me. And the whole class is like, 'Oh yeah, good job Kat.'" Further, in one class discussion, Kat offered stereotypes of female behaviors as her contribution. In discussing *Lord of the Flies*, Kat argues that if the story had been about a group of girls, there would have been much infighting and cattiness. She does not make the connection to the violence that ensues in this novel with the all male character cast.

Although Kat's daily practices demonstrate many of the characteristics of an alpha girl, her understandings of herself and her world do not necessarily confirm that position. In many ways, Kat exemplifies the Girl Power Movement in which girls play with their girliness, their femininity, and simultaneously break gender boundaries and binaries. Kat's reluctance to name herself as an athlete and her understanding of her class contributions and soccer playing as other oriented appear to be traditional female understandings. However, her willingness to put her ideas out there, her lack of interest in traditional displays of femininity, and her playfulness all point to non-traditional female enactments. Perhaps a better way to understand Kat would be to see her as exemplifying Girl Power, but not too much.

Although Kat's life is busy, she does do some personal reading, but even then it is relational. Along with most of her friends ("I don't know anyone who hasn't read them except for like two people. And they want to read them."), Kat loves the *Sisterhood of the Traveling Pants*. Just as the pants travel among all of the characters who are friends, so do the books of the *Sisterhood* series. Kat and her friend Val compare themselves to the female characters and share their views of the various characters.

When asked about the literature that she reads for class, Kat responds that her favorite was *To Kill a Mockingbird*. Her rationale for the *Mockingbird* selection is interesting. Kat claims, "It does have symbolism and I like stuff like that. But it's not as much as *The Lord of the Flies*, and you don't have to analyze it as much."

Molly: Nice girl. In describing whom she is and what she is about, Molly's first comment includes "I like to read books, watch TV, and to hang out with my friends, go shopping, and hang out with my family and take trips." Molly is one of a handful of eighth grade students who when describing themselves included "reader" as an initial descriptor. Further, Molly is particular about what she likes to read. She is enamored with mystery books and selects them based on their covers and then apologizes for that: "I'm kind of bad but I do kind of judge a book by its cover." Her interest in mystery books exclusively, however, precludes her enjoyment of the books read for her eighth grade class. Her favorite selection was To Kill a Mockingbird but that was only because the story contained "more suspense" to it than the others did. However, "when I got into it there was just really nothing to it that I liked." Molly also reads adolescent magazines, subscribes to Seventeen, and purchases Cosmo Girl and Teen People; however, she does not share her reading interests with any of her friends.

During our interview, Molly described herself voluntarily as "nice" without any provoking question. Her nice comment and the fact that she does not engage in any sports or leadership activities speak to her non-alpha status. She maintained that others would describe her as such and defined nice as kind, thoughtful, funny, a good friend, and trustworthy. These traits were difficult to ascertain since Molly rarely talked in class, although she appeared attentive. She stated that she was nervous for any formal presentation. Generally, "I'm not sure if I participate as much. When it's kind of a really serious topic, then I will maybe throw something out but I'm not always raising my hands." When asked why, Molly responded, "I don't know. Maybe I don't want to answer the question wrong." In a relaxed classroom with a teacher who welcomed discussion, Molly's fear of answering incorrectly speaks to her timidity and perhaps the constraints of nice. However, her interest in discussion around "a really serious topic" speaks to the desire of youth to be engaged in worthy discussions. Her interest in serious topics is also revealed when we asked about how she might construct a literature discussion. Molly wants to talk about what she likes and dislikes about the book rather than the symbolism.

Sixth Grade Girls

Raylene: The quiet thinker. Raylene, recently recognized as Student of the Month, spends her time before class reading or silently observing the more active interplay between other students, especially those between boys and girls. She talks about loving different things but is less able to describe them. Instead, she returns to her reading life. In school, she reads (or rereads) the books that the teacher assigns. When given choice, she turns to the classics, setting aside *The Babysitters Club* for *Jane Eyre*. She considers the literature discussion groups "good" and enjoys "meeting to talk about things," but considers some of the questions less than provocative. She talks about trying to turn a question with a "really right answer" into a wider interpretive frame, but being thwarted because of the truly narrow response that the question dictates. She most appreciates discussion group participants who "seem like they really thought about it [the question] and it [their response] was things that you knew—even if I didn't agree with it." She scorns classmates who "were not really serious and would just say something just totally off the wall." She never raised these stances with her peers or her teacher. In fact, the teacher describes her as "someone you have to look for," hesitates to raise her hand, but "the deepest student I've had," exhibiting "amazing thoughts, amazing insight." The students came to this view more slowly. According to the teacher, "once they figured that out, it was like, everything that came out of this student's mouth, they were like, oh, you're so smart, she's so smart, and I want to be in her group because I know it's going to get done right." These students grasped the link between her thinking and her compliance and were then drawn to her.

Marissa: The boisterous socialite. Previously, we briefly introduced you to Marissa. She represents those girls who, unlike Raylene, make their presence known. It often begins when she first walks in the door and calls to her teacher, "Mrs. Riley, Mrs. Riley." She then reports her drama for the day. Once seated, and before class officially begins, she typically takes out a book and reads. In fact, she describes herself as "an active reader" who is "quiet and calmed down" during that time. However, and in her words, "when I'm not reading I'm wild and energetic" and not a "goody two shoes person." Like Raylene, however, she completes assignments and participates in class events according to guidelines established by the teacher. This mindfulness about doing her work and generally following the rules does not prevent her from stealing time to pass notes, acquiring another student's purse for close examination of its contents, heading to the in-class drinking fountain for a brief exchange with friends, and capitalizing on the short walk to it for further surreptitious exchanges with classmates. She describes her time with the literature discussion group as "good" because she "liked that book and I liked how I could compare myself to her." (Her group read *Olive's Ocean.*) She assumes an active role during these group meetings, two times serving as the leader, the person who writes the discussion questions. She mentions the freedom of being in an all-girl group since she finds it "easier to say things." In a mixed group, as true with a whole class exchange, she "wouldn't say things as personal." She also prefers girls because, in her view, "boys don't listen as well." If given the chance to design literature discussion groups, she would allow the "freedom" that she enjoys during the informal conversations she has with friends. Mostly, though, reading is something she does for herself and in private. "That way it's quiet … It bugs me when people talk when I read because it brings me out of the book." While summer vacation typically provides more personal time, that isn't true for Marissa. As she explains, "I'm normally really busy over the summer. When I do read, I go to camp [and mentions a variety of sports camps that she describes as "slumber camps"] … and normally read before I go to bed just to bring me down from all the things of the day." Overall, Marissa represents those girls who are perky and active, accommodate school practices to these personal attributes, and esteem reading more than they engage in it.

Katrina: The emerging alpha girl. Katrina's life is punctuated by taking the lead and taking things on. However, she places each piece in a box. At school, and especially during the literature discussion groups, she is all business. She becomes impatient with peers who stray from the task at hand. She quickly helps to dispense with the completion of the literature discussion assignments in order to move on. For her, this includes huddling with friends not in her group, flipping through the pages of a magazine, talking about the latest basketball game at the local university, or, if in the library, attempting to read her e-mail. In fact, she notes instant messaging as a favorite out-of-school event. Her father's job as the team trainer contributes to her interest in sports and her athletic ways. She plays team sports at school, takes dancing lessons and plays soccer out of school, and reads only if she can become "committed" to the book. The busyness of her out-of-school life and her commitment to completing in-school assignments, many of which include reading but do not entice her to read more, leave scant time and little interest in personal reading.

Results: The Teachers

These teachers, while different in their demeanor and pedagogical choices, care about their students and their educational opportunities. In the eyes of their colleagues and their building principal, they are good teachers. However, their goals and curricular decisions further reduce these girls' opportunities to explore their intellectual selves and reading lives. For example, while sixth grade teacher Sara Riley values students who assert themselves and appreciates girls with a little "sass," the constraints she places on her use of literature discussion groups hamper these opportunities. She assigns roles, specifies the activities for students to complete, and oversees the students' compliance with these predetermined and exact expectations. Kayla Harper, the eighth grade teacher, presents herself as an older version of an alpha girl because she is an acknowledged leader in the school, a coach, and athlete, and is known for her intellect. She does not necessarily encourage that way of being in her classroom. The Honors girls consistently critiqued her wandering discussions while her general track girls praised her story telling. Neither group of girls was necessarily inspired to achieve more in her integrated English/Social Studies classroom. The following vignettes, driven by what we learned across our observations and interviews with these teachers, further highlight their differences as teachers and the contradictory beliefs and stances they project.

Sara Riley: A planner with classroom goals. Sara, whose husband's and dog's pictures adorn her office, evidences a notable fondness for her role as a teacher. In addition to her sixth grade teaching duties, she also coaches volleyball. However, during this observation period, she did not bring the after school duty or family events into her classroom. While she sometimes attempts to soften the behaviors of some girls, especially when they "make a noise of a big sigh along with a drop of the shoulder attitude and make this face," she primarily focuses on the academic task. She notes a preference for those girls who are "just really kind to each other, kind to their classmates, upbeat, and like school." She recognizes the existence of cliques in her school, but does not believe that group membership is "strictly maintained" or that it complicates her intention to have a warm and caring teaching environment. She is aware of girls' general interest in fiction and considers them, as a group, readers. The daily life in her classroom indicates her advance planning of its events and the control she takes of them. For the event that she labels literature discussions, contradictions arise. She chooses the books, forms the groups, creates and assigns roles, and establishes a time line for completing the various specified tasks they include. To make these determinations, she does not have guidelines to follow. Instead, "it's what came together in time for me to start my literature circle." She envisions "little pockets of students just talking about literature and life and whatever. To me, that's the joy of it." This "discussion time" became her main goal. For her students, most often they engaged in "whatever." While she approved the discussion questions to "know that the questions had at least a shot of getting some discussion," the students simply answered them as they did the other assignments linked to this event. While she notes students' interests, she chooses books for convenience (e.g., their availability as book sets or library acquisitions). While she appreciates a girl "a little bit willing to put herself out there and a little bit willing to say something that might offend someone," she neither fosters nor models these attributes. Sara holds good intentions. Students act on them based on their tangled and varied agendas. In the end, the results drift from Sara's hopes and lessen the possibilities for girls to blend their boldness outside of school with their approach to in-school literacy events such as literature discussion groups.

Kayla Harper: Alpha woman. In many ways, Kayla personifies the new alpha girl: smart, confident, athletic, and an acknowledged leader in her middle school. Kayla takes on the administrative leadership role when her principal is out of the building, and her room is an unofficial meeting place during lunch for a dozen or so teachers. Forty-ish with streaked dirty blond hair and with a long distance runner's physique, she dresses fashionably and coaches the high school girls' track team. Kayla was hired as the eighth grade English/Social Studies block teacher seven years ago and teaches both honors and general track sections of this integrated course. Kayla explained that she was a history major with an English minor but that her history focus was on civil rights in America. Her educational intellectual interest is in how socioeconomic class plays out in schools. She is currently taking courses to receive her certificate in school administration and expresses an ongoing interest in issues of equity, particularly as they relate to social class, race, and gender.

This interest in equity issues is found in her book selections. In discussing her selections, she details the thought process that she addresses. First, she does not want to be redundant with what students read at the high school nor with the style and content of the books. Because her students read *Animal Farm* currently, she could not justify including *Watership Down* because it was another book with talking animals. Generally, she uses the books to complement and extend her social studies concepts. For example, *Our Only May Amelia* presents a coming of age story of a young white girl in the Northwest whose life is circumscribed by her gender. Another example, *Nisei Daughter,* explores the life of a Japanese adolescent whose Seattle family is forced to live in Japanese relocation camps during World War II when anti-Japanese sentiment is rampant.

Kayla claims that she uses a literature circle discussion approach, although our field notes revealed little evidence of the traditional concept of literature circles. Kayla had her students work in small groups, but the tasks vary and typically involve some kind of creative project. Since the tasks involve coming "to consensus on some of the concrete items like main characters, plot, conflict, all of those things," Kayla frames them as literature discussion groups.

She characterizes girls in her eighth grade classrooms as those who are "seriously thinking about dates and dances and boys" to those "who are already gearing toward taking the SAT and scholarships and progressing in academics and careers and jobs." She says that girls, as compared to boys, generally are "passionate about a cause. I find more girls interested in the environment or animal rights." Further, she notes that girls at this middle school dominate the school leadership positions, which is a nationwide trend. She worries about girls who "uh, heavy makeup coming on, lots of more provocative clothing and … that's the split. When that happens, boy, it's hard to reclaim. Because all of their value is on how they are seen by others and not on what they think about themselves."

Interestingly enough, Kayla's pedagogical practices do not necessarily exemplify her alpha girl beliefs. Although her curriculum, including her reading selections, certainly focuses on issues of equity, her own daily classroom practices exemplified a traditional, teacher-centered approach. As our field notes revealed and students' comments asserted, Kayla talked about her family and her own life an inordinate amount of time and engaged in discussions that wandered far from curricular topics. One Honors student noted that if your mind wandered during class discussions, you would have no idea how the topic jumped into the new realm. Another Honors student asked aloud during the showing of a clip from the classic movie *Funny Girl* what this movie had to do with their study of the Beat Poets, and was not offered an explanation. Usually, Honors students were much more critical of these kinds of practices than the general track students who saw Kayla as a personable teacher who made the learning of English more enjoyable.

Teachers Mentoring Girls

As the previous vignettes indicate, these teachers differ in their design of their language arts classrooms. Sara directs her classroom without making herself its leading character. In this more off-to-the-side role, students have the unrealized opportunity to play with putting their ideas forward, contribute to the direction of a large or small group discussion, and contend with comments that challenge or contradict their ideas. In a way, the constraints that Sara imposes also afford safeguards. She expects students to be civil and respectful. She encourages the quiet students and is willing to muffle the more boisterous and demanding.

In contrast, Kayla is always at the center of her classroom, regaling students with personal anecdotes and leading the discussion to topics that she believes are always of worth, issues of equity and social justice. While this focus certainly warrants continual exploration, Kayla does not allow its exploration. Instead, she constructs a curriculum and pedagogy where she remains the focal point and her views are the ones that take center stage. As previously asserted, Kayla presents herself as an older version of an alpha girl—a leader, an athlete and coach, and an intellectual. Like Kat, she thrives on attention, and uses her role as teacher to claim it.

Neither teacher truly takes on the attributes so central to literature discussion groups that could further girls' (and their male classmates') opportunities to combine deep thinking with their personal lives and experiences. The chances for choice go away and the opportunities to flex independence in the direction of their learning opportunities remain minimal. These decisions, in turn, diminish these teachers' influence on the burgeoning robustness of girls' out of school lives. As Wexler (1992) noted, the work of adolescence is about "becoming somebody" and that work becomes more complicated in classrooms that do not support ways to create a wholeness that allows girlishness, intellectual boldness, and a unified presentation of the many facets of their lives.

While not all alpha girls, the girls' profiles evidence bits and pieces of them. The academic possibilities afforded by true literature discussions or book club formats offer the chance to lead the way in supporting the new directions of these girls' lives. In these classrooms, that possibility remains suppressed.

Discussion and Educational Significance

Young women, often deemed to be alpha girls and can-do girls, are being framed as the face of the future. Yet, Brumberg (2002) captures an underlying tension: "Despite the important and satisfying gains women have made in achieving greater access to education, power, and all forms of self-expression, including sexual, we have a sense of disquiet about what has happened to our girls" (p. 5). We unveil some explanations for this disquiet.

Some of this disquiet stems from the entanglement of these girls' definitions of themselves and the girls they become in a classroom setting. Girls, like Raylene, with heady proclivities are reduced to participation in simple-minded conversations. Others, like most of the girls in this study, desire to read but lack school and personal time to do much of it. Others, who verge on becoming true readers, are assigned texts that too often dampen rather than increase their enthusiasm to read.

The teachers' actions also contribute to a sense of disquiet. For the teachers in this investigation, their professed interest and use of events like literature discussion groups or book clubs do not materialize. In teachers like Sara, we see a variation that lessens the promise of rich interactions with text and reduces students' chances for finding pleasure in reading. For Kayla and too many others, they simply lose sight of what they say they do in favor of what appears to be a more personal agenda.

We did not intend to propose paths for teachers or the girls in their classrooms to follow. Instead, we framed each research question as a quest for meaning about girls and their participation in literature discussion groups. We do believe that the findings from this research point to the challenges that remain in framing classroom events such as literature discussion groups in ways that increase rather than dampen girls' growth as women and readers. We also believe that girls' lives are more complicated and nuanced than an alpha girl existence.

In the classic movie, *Butch Cassidy and the Sundance Kid*, Sundance chides Butch to "just keep thinking." We commiserate with Butch's response that he has vision while others wear bifocals. We, like others, hold a vision of the possibility where schools and their teachers nurture girls' new sense of themselves in ways that promote independence, savvy, and the joy of reading. Like Freire (2004), we wait "patiently impatiently" (p. xxix). We look forward to replacing our disquiet with "quietism" (p. 8). To that end, we hope that our initial foray into these two worlds of girls and reading encourages others with, again in the words of Freire, "dreams toward whose realization we struggle" (p. 7). We envision a future where girls are nurtured in school and in their communities to find their own path. Rather than strive to be somebody else's shadow, these girls would hold the possibility to become more than those girls whom Kindlon (2006) touts— not just girls who embody the laudable features typically framed and acquired by gender membership, but who also read voraciously and well along the way.

References

Adams, N. G. (1999). Fighting to be somebody: The discursive practices of girls fighting. *Educational Studies, 30*, 115–139.

Adams, N. G., & Bettis, P. J. (2003). Commanding the room in short skirts: Cheering as the embodiment of ideal girlhood. *Gender & Society, 17*(1), 73–91.

Almasi, J. (1995). The nature of fourth graders' sociocognitive conflicts in peer-led and teacher-led discussions of literature. *Reading Research Quarterly, 30*, 314–351.

Alvermann, D., Commeyras, M., Young, J., Randall, S., & Hinson, D. (1997). Interrupting gendered discursive practices in classroom talk about texts: Easy to think about, difficult to do. *Journal of Literacy Research, 29*(1), 73–104.

American Association of University Women. (1992). *How schools shortchange girls: The AAUW Report*. Washington, DC: American Association of University Women Educational Foundation.

American Association of University Women. (1998). *Gender gaps: Where schools still fail our children*. Washington, DC: American Association of University Women Educational Foundation.

Appleman, D. (2006). *Reading for themselves: How to transform adolescents into lifelong readers through out-of-class book clubs*. Portsmouth, NH: Heinemann.

Barbieri, M. (1995). *Sounds from the heart: Learning to listen to girls*. Portsmouth, NH: Heinemann.

Bettis, P. J., & Adams, N. G. (2005). *Geographies of girlhood: Identities in-between*. Mahwah, NJ: Erlbaum.

Blackford, V. H. (2004). *Out of this world: Why literature matters to girls*. New York: Teachers College Press.

Brown, L. M., & Gilligan, C. (1992). *Meeting at the crossroads: Women's psychology and girls' development*. Cambridge, MA: Harvard University Press.

Brumberg, J. J. (2002). Introduction. In L. Greenfield, *Girl culture* (p. 5). San Francisco: Chronicle Books.

Budgeon, S. (1998). "I'll tell you what I really, really want": Girl power and self-identity in Britain. In S. Inness (Ed.), *Millennium girls: Today's girls around the world* (pp. 115–144). Lanham, MD: Rowman & Littlefield.

Daniels, H. (1994). *Literature circles: Voice and choice in the student-centered classroom.* York, ME: Stenhouse.

Davies, B. (1989). *Frogs and snails and feminist tales: Preschool children and gender.* Sydney: Allen & Unwin.

Davies, B. (1993). *Shards of glass: Children reading and writing beyond gendered identity.* Cresskill, NJ: Hampton Press.

Davies, B. (2000). *A body of writing 1990–1999.* New York: AltaMira Press.

Denzin, N., & Lincoln, Y. S. (2005). *Handbook of qualitative research.* Thousand Oaks, CA: Sage.

Devault, M. (1996). Talking back to sociology: Distinctive contributions of feminist methodology. *Annual Review of Sociology, 22,* 29–44.

Eeds, M., & Wells, D. (1989). Grand conversations: An exploration of meaning construction in literature study groups. *Research in the Teaching of English, 23,* 4–29.

Fine, M., & Weis, L. (1998). Writing the 'wrongs' of fieldwork: Confronting our own research/ writing dilemmas in urban ethnographies. In G. Shacklock & J. Smyth (Eds.), *Being reflexive in critical educational and social research* (pp. 13–35). Bristol, PA: Falmer Press.

Freire, P. (2004). *Pedagogy of indignation.* Boulder, CO: Paradigm.

Gall, J. P., Gall, M. D., & Borg, W. R. (2005). *Applying educational research.* New York: Allyn & Bacon.

Goatley, V. J., Brock, C. H., & Raphael, T. E. (1995). Diverse learners participating in regular education "Book Clubs." *Reading Research Quarterly, 30,* 352–380.

Harris, A. (2004a). *All about the girl: Culture, power and identity.* New York: Routledge.

Harris, A. (2004b). *Future girl: Young women in the twenty-first century.* New York: Routledge.

Hinchman, K. A., Payne-Bourcy, L., Thomas, H., & Olcott, K. C. (2002). Representing adolescents' literacies: Case studies of three white males. *Reading Research and Instruction, 41*(3), 229–246.

Hull, G., & Schultz, K. (Eds.). (2002). *School's out: Bridging out-of-school literacies with classroom practice.* New York: Teachers College Press.

Hunter, J. (2002). *How young ladies became girls.* New Haven, CT: Yale University Press.

Inness, S. (1998). *Millennium girls: Today's girls around the world.* Lanham, MD: Rowman & Littlefield.

Inness, S. (1999). *Tough girls: Women warriors and wonder women in popular culture.* Philadelphia: University of Pennsylvania Press.

Irvin, J., & Rycik, J. (Eds.). (2001). *What adolescents deserve: A commitment to students' literacy learning.* Newark, DE: International Reading Association.

Jones, S. (2006). *Girls, social class, and literacy: What teachers can do to make a difference.* Portsmouth, NH: Heinemann.

Kenway, J., & Willis, S. (1998). *Answering back: Girls, boys, and feminism in schools.* London: Routledge.

Kindlon, D. (2006). *Alpha girls: Understanding the new American girl and how she is changing the world.* New York: Rodale.

Langer, J. A. (1995). *Envisioning literature: Literary understanding and literature instruction.* New York: Teachers College Press.

Lancy, D. F. (1993). *Qualitative research in education.* New York: Longman.

Lather, P. (1991). *Getting smart: Feminist research and pedagogy within/in the postmodern.* New York: Routledge.

Lave, J., & Wegner, E. (1991). *Situated learning: Legitimate peripheral participation.* New York: University Press.

LeCompte, M. D., Millroy, W. L., & Preissle, J. (Eds.). (1992). *The handbook of qualitative research in education.* New York: Academic Press.

Marshall, C. (1997). *Feminist critical policy analysis: A perspective from primary and secondary schooling.* London: Falmer Press.

Marshall, C. (1999). Researching the margins: Feminist critical policy analysis. *Educational Policy, 13*(1–2), 59–76.

Marshall, C., & Rossman, G. B. (1989). *Designing qualitative research.* Newbury Park, CA: Sage.

McRobbie, A. (1993). Shut up and dance: Youth culture and changing modes of femininity. *Cultural Studies, 7,* 406–426.

Mitchell, S. (1995). *The new girl: Girls' culture in England 1889–1915.* New York: Columbia University Press.

Nelson, C., & Vallone, L. (Eds.). (1994). *The girl's own: Cultural histories of the Anglo-American girl, 1830–1915.* Athens, GA: University of Georgia Press.

Orenstein, P. (1994). *Schoolgirls: Young women, self esteem, and the confidence gap.* New York: Doubleday.

Perkins, L. R. (2005). *Criss cross.* New York: Greenwillow Books.

Pipher, M. (1995). *Reviving Ophelia: Saving the selves of adolescent girls.* New York: Ballantine Books.

Qualis Research Associates. (1998). *The Ethnograph v50.* Denver, CO: Qualis.

Roe, M. F. (2004). Literacy for middle school students: Challenges of cultural synthesis. *Research in Middle Level Education Online, 28*(1). Retrieved February 8, 2004, from http:// www.nmsa.org/

Rosenblatt, L. M. (1978). *The reader, the text, and the poem.* Carbondale, IL: Southern Illinois University Press.

Schratz, M. (Ed.). (1993). *Qualitative voices in educational research.* Washington, DC: Falmer Press.

Smith, S. A. (2000). Talking about real stuff: Explorations of agency and romance in an all-girls' Book Club. *Language Arts, 78*(1), 30–38.

Smith, M., & Wilhelm, J. (2002). *Reading don't fix no Chevys: Literacy in the lives of young men.* Portsmouth, NH: Heinemann.

Spinelli, J. (2000). *Stargirl.* New York: Alfred A. Knopf.

Taylor, J. M, Gilligan, C., & Sullivan, A. M. (1995). *Between voice and silence: Women and girls, race and relationship.* Cambridge, MA: Harvard University Press.

Walkerdine, V. (1990). *Schoolgirl fictions.* London: Verso.

Walkerdine, V. (1993). Girlhood through the looking glass. In M. de Ras & M. Lunenberg (Eds.), *Girls, girlhood, and girls' studies in transition* (pp. 9–25). Amsterdam: Het Spinhuis.

Wexler, P. (1992). *Becoming somebody: Toward a social psychology of school.* Washington, DC: Falmer Press.

Appendix A: Interview Protocol for Student Participants
An Introduction

I am interested in learning from you about how you describe yourself as a young woman in middle school and as a reader. I'm particularly interested in hearing you talk about your participation in your class's discussions about the books you read. In fact, sometimes I may ask about specific events that I have observed. While I will share your comments with my research team member, I am the only one who will know that the comments came from you. Then, so I can concentrate on what you're saying, I would like your permission to tape record our conversation. Is that OK with you?

Exploring Adolescent Girl and Reader Identity

Tell me about yourself. (Clarify as necessary: Just tell me who you are. If you were describing yourself, what would you say? Use prompts to tease out in and outside of school personas that include group membership and affiliation.)

Do you consider yourself to be a nice girl? What does that mean to you and other girls in this school? Tell me about yourself as a reader.

How does the description of yourself as a person fit into how you describe yourself as a reader?

Exploring the Relationship of Adolescent Girl, Reader
Identity, and Literature Discussion Group Behaviors

Before talking with you about the literature discussions, tell me about the books you use. (Probes: titles, selection process)

How would you describe your participation in your language arts class when you talk about books?

During our first interview, you told me about yourself. Is that what you're like during this time?

Think of people whose participation during discussions you admire. What are they like? What do they do during these discussions that makes you admire them? (Tease out gendered qualities using probing questions.)

Think of people whose participation during book discussions you don't admire. What are they like? What specific things do they do?

What do you do during book discussions that you like about yourself? Of those things, which do you like best?

What does your teacher do during literature discussion groups. What do you like and don't like about what she does?

If you were to design a book discussion, what would it be like? Who would be members? What would you read?

Sometimes my friends and I chat about books over the phone or using e-mail. Do you ever do that? Have you thought about it? Do you think it would work?

Is there anything else you would like me to know about you as a participant in a book discussion that my previous questions didn't cover?

Appendix B: Interview Protocol for Teachers
An Introduction

(Remind the teacher that his or her identity will remain anonymous. Receive his or her permission to audiotape.) "In this interview, I want to better understand your views of girls' behaviors during your book discussions. I have a few prepared questions to initially guide our conversations." (For each question use probes as appropriate to follow their lead and deepen their responses.)

- Tell me about the girls in your class. How do you see these girls as readers?
- Tell me about the nice girls in your class. Do they exhibit differences as readers?
- Before talking with you about the literature discussions, tell me about the books you use.
- (Probes: titles, selection process)
- Tell me about your typical literature discussion groups. How do you describe your role?
- What roles do the girls play during the discussion groups? Do these differ from the boys' roles?
- Do you see differences based on peer group affiliation?
- How would you describe the ideal literature discussion group?
- How would you describe the ideal girl's participation during this discussion?
- How would you describe the girl who falls short of this ideal?
- Is there anything that these questions didn't cover that you want me to understand about your class's literature discussions and your female students' participation in them?
- What challenges and excites you as a teacher during the literature discussion groups?
- As I've observed, I've wondered about a few things. (Insert questions driven by the observations that link to girls' behaviors or the teacher's responses.)
- What are the most important things you want me to know about your literature discussion groups and your girls' participation in them?

Appendix C: Observation Codes

Teacher

- Task explanation of teacher TET8H TET8G TET6C1 TET6C2
- Teacher formal talk (due dates, behavior, expectations) TFT 8H TFT8G TFT6C1 TFT6C2
- Teacher gender talk TGT8H TGT8G TGT6C1 TGT6C2
- Teacher race talk TRT8H TRT8G TRT6C1 TRT6C2

- Teacher humor TH8H TH8G TH6C1 TH6C2
- Student task explanation STE(M/F)8H STE(M/F)8G STE(M/F)6C1 STE(M/F)6C2
- Student social behaviors SSB(M/F)8H SSB(M/F)8G SSB(M/F)6C1 SSB(M/F)6C2
- Student identity presenters (appearance descriptors) SIP(M/F)8H SIP(M/F)8G SIP(M/F)6C1 SIP(M/F)6C2
- Teacher tracking talk TTT8H TTT8G TTT6C1 TTT6C2
- Teacher evaluation TE8H TE8G TE6C1 TE6C2
- Teacher question TQ8H TQ8G TQ6C1 TQ6C2
- Teacher task behaviors (an act) TTB8H TTB8G TTB6C1 TTB6C2
- Teacher social behaviors (e.g., call from husband) TSB8H TSB8G TSB6C1 TSB6C2

Student (add Male or Female)

- Student response (an action) SR(M/F)8H SR(M/F)8G SR(M/F)6C1 SR(M/F)6C2
- Student task behaviors STB(M/F)8H STB(M/F)8G STB(M/F)6C1 STB(M/F)6C2
- Student off task behaviors SOTB(M/F)8H SOTB(M/F)8G SOTB(M/F)6C1 SOTB(M/F)6C2
- Teacher conversation linked to school tasks TCS8H TCS8G TCS6C1 TCS6C2
- Teacher conversation not linked to school tasks TCSN8H TCSN8G TCSN6C1 TCSN6C2
- Student questions SQ(M/F)8H SQ(M/F)8G SQ(M/F)6C1 SQ(M/F)6C2
- Student answer (a response to a question) SA(M/F)8H SA(M/F)8G SA(M/F)6C1 SA(M/F)6C2
- Student conversation linked to school tasks but conversational SCS(M/F)8H SCS(M/F)8G SCS(M/F)6C1 SCS(M/F)6C2

Note: The letters provide shorthand for the longer code while the numbers denote a grade level and section. For the following:

Student conversation not linked to school tasks	Student reading	Student reading (not part of curriculum)
$SCSN(M/F)8H$	$SR(M/F)8H$	$SRN(M/F)8H$
$SCSN(M/F)8G$	$SR(M/F)8G$	$SRN(M/F)8G$
$SCSN(M/F)6C_1$	$SR(M/F)6C_1$	$SRN(M/F)6C_1$
$SCSN(M/F)6C_2$	$SR(M/F)6C_2$	$SRN(M/F)6C_2$
Student humor	Student gender talk (gender is mentioned or the topic links to gender)	Group task conversation
$SH(M/F)8H$	$SGT(M/F)8H$	$GTC(M/F)8H$
$SH(M/F)8G$	$SGT(M/F)8G$	$GTC(M/F)8G$
$SH(M/F)6C_1$	$SGT(M/F)6C_1$	$GTC(M/F)6C_1$
$SH(M/F)6C_2$	$SGT(M/F)6C_2$	$GTC(M/F)6C_2$

Events

Night of the Notables (Grade 8 only)	Television watching	Question response segment
NN8H	TV8H	QR8H
NN8G	TV8G	QR8G
	$TV6C_1$	$QR6C_1$
	$TV6C_2$	$QR6C_2$
Literature discussion group (Grade 6 only)	Book discussion group with the whole class	
$LDG6C_1$	BDWC8H	
$LDG6C_2$	BDWC8G	
	$BDWC6C_1$	
	$BDWC6C_2$	

example QR8H refers to the question response segment code for the eighth grade honors section while $TV6C_2$ refers to television watching for the first grade 6 section.

Appendix D: Interview Codes

Identity: Age, grade, adjectives ID8H ID8G ID6C1 ID6C2

- Identity: Things I do IA8H IA8G IA6
- Identity: Friendship groups IFG8H IFG8G IFG6C1 IFG6C2
- Nice: Definition, identification with NICE8H NICE8G NICE6C1 NICE6C2
- Ideal girl IDEAL8H IDEAL8G IDEAL6C1 IDEAL6C2
- Personal reading: Identify (a reader or not) PRI8H   PRI8G PRI6C1 PRI6C2
- Personal reading: Genre and examples (genre and/or titles) PRG8H PRG8G PR6C1 PR6C2
- Personal reading: Influences (personal reading recommendations) PRIF8H PRIF8G PRIF6C1 PRIF6C2
- Personal reading: Reading practices (when, conditions, outside and inside choices, summer reading, chat with friends) PRP8H PRP8G PRP6C1 PRP6C2
- Personal reading: Gender issues (girl/reader connections) PRGE8H PRGE8G PRGE6C1 PRGE6C2
- School reading (assigned texts): Comments across books, preferences about how they are expected to read them SRG8H SRG8G SRG6C1 SRG6C2
- School reading: Comments about a book or combination of books SRS8H SRS8G SRS6C1 SRS6C2
- Class participation: How they describe their participation CPP8H CPP8G CPP6C1 CPP6C2
- Class participation: People they admire and reasons CPA8H CPA8G CPA6C1 CPA6C2
- Class participation: People they don't admire CPD8H CPD8G CPD6C1 CPD6C2
- Class participation: Teacher comments—positive CPTA8H CPTA8G CPTA6C1 CPTA6C2
- Class participation: Teacher comments—negative CPTNA8H CPTNA8G CPTNA6C1 CPTNA6C2
- Kid designed book curriculum: What they would do if they were in charge KDBC8H KDBC8G KDBC6C1 KDBC6C2

Note: The letters provide shorthand for the longer code while the numbers denote a grade level and section. For example PRG8H refers to personal reading references for the eighth grade honors section while PR6C1 refers to personal reading references in the first section of grade 6.

ARTICLE 3: THE EFFECT OF SCHOOL UNIFORM ON INCIDENTAL PHYSICAL ACTIVITY AMONG 10-YEAR-OLD CHILDREN

Authors: Hannah Norrish, Fiona Farringdon, Max Bulsara, and Beth Hands
Affiliation: School of Health Sciences, University of Notre Dame Australia, Fremantle, Australia

The school setting provides a unique opportunity to promote physical activity in children by ensuring adequate time, appropriate facilities and education guidance is offered. However school uniform design could also limit physical activity. A repeated measures crossover design was used to compare school recess and lunchtime physical activity over four weeks in 64 primary school children (M = 10.48 yrs) when wearing winter uniform or sports uniform. Pedometers recorded step counts during each school recess and lunch break. Perception of the level of intensity of physical activity was also measured using a self-report log book. Mixed model analyses found that girls, but not boys, were significantly more active at recess (p=.03), lunch (p = .04) and overall (p = .006) when wearing their sports uniform compared to their winter uniform. School uniform did not impact the boy's physical activity levels. Perceived intensity of physical activity increased slightly among both girls and boys. A physically restrictive school uniform has the potential to inhibit physical activity among primary-school-aged girls.

Keywords: children; physical activity; school uniform; incidental breaks; pedometer; gender difference

Introduction

The school environment provides an important opportunity to enhance daily physical activity in children. The school day includes formal physical activity opportunities such as physical education and sport as well as unstructured play time during recess and lunchtime breaks. Activity undertaken during these important play breaks is discretionary and children best accumulate activity when they are able to interact with their peers in an outdoors setting (Pate, Baranowski, Dowda, & Trost, 1996). These school breaks generally comprise a recess of approximately 15 minutes and lunch break of approximately 30–40 minutes and therefore provide important opportunities for children to meet a significant proportion of the recommended daily physical activity level of 60 minutes (Department of Health and Aging, 2004). Data collected during the 2007 Australian National Children's Nutrition and Physical Activity Survey showed that approximately 20 minutes of lunch breaks were spent engaged in moderate to vigorous activity in a sample of 794 10- to 13-year-old children (Stanley, Ridley, & Olds, 2011). Beighle, Alderman, Morgan, and Le Masurier (2008) found that children spent more than 60% of their recess time in physical activity compared to outside school time (20%) and Loucaides and Jago (2008) found that recess activity alone accounted for 9% of daily physical activity.

Gender differences in physical activity level and intensity are consistently reported across numerous studies regardless of the measurement protocol. Sallis, Prochaska, and Taylor (2000) reviewed 1089 studies that evaluated 40 variables that impact on physical activity levels in children aged 3 to 12 years. In 81% of gender comparisons, boys were more active than girls. Pedometry is the most common objective measure of physical activity in the school setting. Morgan, Graser, and Pangrazi (2008) found that late elementary and junior high girls took approximately 10% fewer steps per day than boys. Tudor-Locke, Williams, Reis, and Pluto (2006) studied Year 6 children and reported that boys took significantly more total steps per day than girls especially during recess, lunch and after school. Of interest to this present study, Loucaides and Jago (2008) found that the largest differences in steps between boys and girls were observed during the 20 minute recess period.

These differences could be due in part to intensity of preferred activities. Boys and girls appear to use their play periods to engage in different activities (Harper & Sanders, 1975). Numerous researchers have reported that boys participate in more total games, ball games, chase games and rough and tumble activities than girls (Cratty, Ikeda, Martin, Jennett, & Morris, 1970; Hands, Parker & Larkin, 2006; Pellegrini, Blatchford, Kato, & Baines, 2004; Pfister, 1993; Reilly & Stratton, 1995). Girls are more likely to play more jumping/verbal games, such as jump rope and clapping/chanting games. The intensity of these activities range from light to vigorous, and overall time engaged in moderate to vigorous physical activity during school break times may not be optimal. For example, Zask, Beurden, Barnett, Brooks, & Dietrich (2001) found that of 500 kindergarten to Year 6 children, only 50% of the boys and 28.6% girls engaged in moderate to vigorous physical activity in most break periods. Hands, Parker, Glasson, Brinkman, and Read (2004) found that more females engaged in low intensity physical activity such as standing or walking around during recess (20.2%) and lunch (12.4%) compared with males during recess (8.9%) and lunch (4.5%).

Schools present a unique opportunity to provide time, facilities and guidance for children to participate in physical activity and contribute largely to meeting recommended daily physical activity levels (World Health Organization, 2008). However, some school rules, policies or physical environments may act as either barriers or motivators to physical activity. Previous school-based structural interventions shown to increase children's physical activity during play breaks include fitness sessions (Scruggs, Beveridge, & Watson, 2003), structured games (Connolly & McKenzie, 1995), provision of play-ground markings (Stratton, 2000; Stratton & Leonard, 2002; Stratton & Mota, 2000), loose equipment (Afonso & Botelho, 2003; Verstraete, Cardon, DeClercq, & Bourdeaudhuij, 2006), fixed equipment (Sut-terby & Frost, 2002), improved design of the playground (Afonso & Botelho, 2003; Ridgers, Stratton, Fairclough, & Twisk, 2007; Stratton & Leonard, 2002), length of play break (Verstraete, Cardon, DeClercq, and Bourdeaudhuij, 2006; Zask, Beurden, Barnett, Brooks, & Diet-rich, 2001) and teacher prompts (McKenzie et al., 1997; Sallis et al., 2001). On the other hand, barriers to physical activity include limited availability of play space or lack of playground markings (Stratton, 2000; Stratton & Leonard, 2002), and restrictive school rules and poli-cies, such as insufficient sports equipment and length of scheduled eating time and play time (Marron, 2008). Marron (2008) found that 19.9% of schools did not provide equipment during incidental breaks due to limited storage space, high equipment costs or risk of equip-ment loss/damage. Further, many schools did not permit students to bring their own sporting equipment to school.

One potential barrier that has not been explicitly explored, yet an-ecdotally observed, is the requirement by some schools for students to wear school uniforms that may restrict free movement. In many independent Australian schools, the standard winter uniform for boys consists of long- or short-sleeve buttoned-up shirts, tie, jump-er, long trousers, and leather shoes. For girls, the uniform consists of similar upper body attire, however they wear a knee-length skirt or pinafore and stockings with their leather shoes. The summer uniform for boys comprises shorts, short-sleeve shirt and leather shoes; for girls it consists of a belted tunic or short-sleeve shirt and lightweight skirt which are less physically restrictive. Overall how-ever, such school uniforms are not designed for students to partici-pate in moderate or vigorous physical activity. In contrast, the sports uniform consists of shorts or tracksuit pants, a t-shirt and tracksuit top, combined with sports shoes for both sexes. However children are only permitted to wear this on physical education or sports days. Some studies have found that children's physical activity levels differ significantly throughout the course of the year (Beighle et al., 2008, Kohl & Hobbs, 1998). In Mediterranean climates, children tend to be more active during summer than winter (Loucaides, Chedzoy, & Bennett, 2003; Rowland & Hughes, 2006). As seasonality may impact on children's physical activity levels, it would be of interest to examine if the design of school uniforms contributes towards this trend. In many Australian schools, winter uniforms, particularly for girls, appear to be more restrictive than summer uniforms, and therefore may discourage physical activity.

Some researchers have reported complaints by girls that clothing can be a barrier to being more physically active. Biddle et al. (2005) found that adolescent girls felt inhibited from cycling to school because they were required to wear a skirt as part of the school uniform. Others did not participate in school sport due to tight, ill-fitting or inappropriate clothing (Coakley & White, 1992; Hands, et al., 2004, Orme, 1991; Porter, 2002). However, few studies have investigated the impact of clothing attire, and more specifically school uniform, on children's physical activity and intensity.

The purpose of the study was to examine the effect of school uniform on the amount, and perceived intensity of physical activity, undertaken by 10-year-old children during play breaks at school. We hypothesized that the children would be more active, particularly the girls, when wearing their sports uniform compared to their school winter uniform. We also hypothesized that the children would engage in more vigorous activity when wearing the sports uniform compared to the winter uniform. Reflecting on school rules and policies in the context of physical activity is crucial if physical activity is to be encouraged. Therefore, how 'active friendly' the school uniform is for playing during incidental breaks should be considered (Department of Education, 2012).

Methods

This pilot study used a repeated measures crossover design to compare school recess and lunchtime physical activity over four weeks in Year Six primary school children when wearing winter uniform or sports uniform. The study was conducted in term two of the school year, beginning at the start of June when students change to winter school uniform; in part to minimize the effect of adverse weather conditions.

In Weeks 1 and 3 participants wore their standard winter school uniform and in Weeks 2 and 4, participants wore their sports uniform.

Participants

The participants were 64 children (males = 36, females = 28) with a mean age of 10.48 yrs (SD = .53). This convenience sample comprised students in the two Year 6 classes attending a small independent metropolitan primary school. Once permission was obtained from the principal and teachers at the school, all Year 6 students were invited to participate in the study via information sheets and letters to parents. Active parent and student consent was obtained from 98.46% of the sample. Only one student declined to participate. This study was approved by the Institutional Human Research Ethics Committee.

Measures and Procedures Physical Activity

Yamax Digi-Walker SW200 pedometers were used to record the number of steps taken during recess and lunchtime each day. This model is a valid and reliable measure of physical activity among children (Barfield, Rowe, & Michael, 2004; Bassett et al., 2000) and four or five days is sufficient time to obtain a reliable mean step count (Gretebeck & Montoye, 1992; Trost, Pate, Freedson, Sallis, & Taylor, 2000). At the beginning of the study, each pedometer was tested for accuracy by completion of a 20-step test (Tudor-Locke, Williams, Reis, & Pluto, 2002). During the data collection, a team of 10 adults retested each pedometer on the Sunday prior to each week (Sidman, Vincent, Corbin, Pangrazi, & Vincent, 2001).

The data were collected by trained students from the Year 7 class. They were shown how to ensure all pedometers were working, how to seal the pedometers with stickers to record data after each break. All pedometers were numbered so that each student used the same pedometer during all four data-collection weeks. During a briefing before the study, all participants were shown how to ensure pedometers were fastened 2-3 inches to the right of their navels, in line with the midpoint of the right knee, and on the waistband of their pants/shorts/skirts.

Approximately five minutes before each play break, the research assistants distributed pedometer boards to the Year 6 classrooms. Pedometers were worn for 20 minutes during recess and 35 minutes during lunch. Both breaks had a warning bell 5 minutes prior to the end of the break. At that time, students put away any play equipment and started to return to class. Actual activity time, therefore, was calculated as 15 minutes for recess and 20 minutes for lunch, as students were required to sit and eat their lunch for the first 10 minutes of lunchtime. At the conclusion of each break, the students reattached their pedometer to their number on the pedometer board. The research assistants recorded step data against each pedometer number in a record book and resealed the pedometers in preparation for the next break. The participants also recorded if they lost their pedometer and the type of uniform they were wearing in their log book.

Perceived Intensity of Physical Activity

Perceived intensity of physical activity was recorded in a log book by the student immediately after each break. Diary measures and log books have the strongest validity of 18 self-report methods of assessment on physical activity in children (Sallis, 1991; Sirard & Pate, 2001). In this study, a simple scale of faces rated one to three was used with $1 =$ light physical activity (no huffing and puffing), $2 =$ moderate physical activity (some huffing and puffing), and $3 =$ vigorous activity (lots of huffing and puffing) (see Figure 1). The face validity of the log book designed for this study was confirmed by a team of experts in measurement of physical activity then piloted and modified with a small group of primary school children. The Year 6 teachers used a set protocol to prompt completion. These scores were converted into a mean perceived-intensity score for each uniform condition (maximum 3, minimum 1).

Data Collection

Data were collected at recess and lunch over the four-week period, with a potential maximum of 10 days (10 recess and 10 lunch occasions) for each uniform condition. The data for the first day were

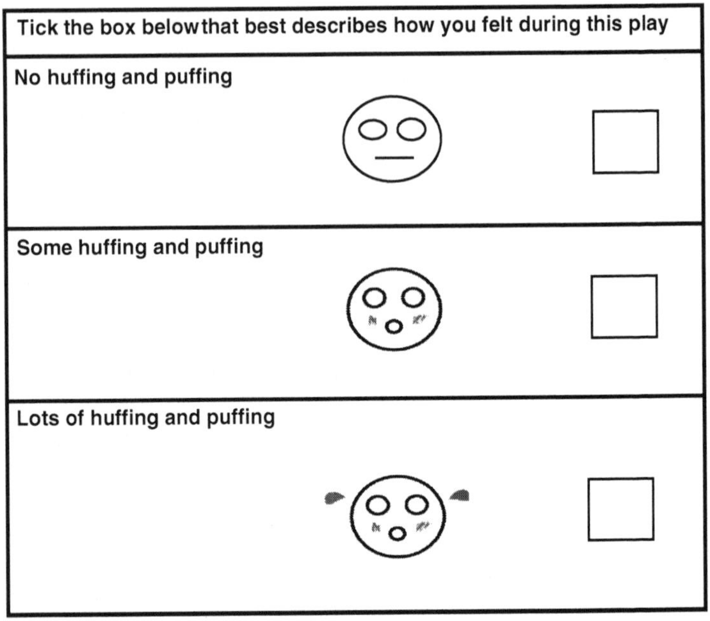

Figure 1 Perceived intensity scale.

not included to minimize the effect of reactivity, and data were not gathered on four days due to inclement weather during Week 4 when the participants were wearing sports uniform. In addition, data were missing due to children being absent, kept in class to finish work or as a consequence of poor behavior, getting injured or falling ill, going on a school excursion, being removed from the playground due to the 'no hat, no play' rule, or the weather being unfavourable for outdoors play. The final number of data points for participants ranged between 4 and 15 for winter uniform and 2 and 12 for summer uniform.

Data Analysis

Data were excluded if the pedometer malfunctioned; was taken off for over five minutes; lost; if the student wore the incorrect uniform; or did not provide at least four days data for each uniform type. In addition, pedometer data were removed if the recorded step counts were below 100 or over 2000 during recess or below 150 and over 3000 during lunch as these were considered to be unusually high or low step counts and therefore considered as outliers. For these data, the responses for individuals were tracked to see if there was a pattern before exclusion. Consequently the final sample sizes varied each day and between recess and lunch throughout the study. Differences in perceived intensity between gender, uniform type and occasion were examined using t-tests. A linear mixed model was used to quantify the relationship between the number of pedometer steps (the dependent variable), uniform type, play breaks (recess or lunch) for the whole sample and stratified by gender. This model can account for repeated observations taken over time (Singer & Willett, 2003). Uniform and Incidental Breaks were treated as fixed effect parameters and a post-hoc test was carried out to compare the mean changes in number of steps over time. Statistical analysis was carried out using SPSS v. 18 utilizing the mixed procedure and the level of significance was set at $p = .05$.

Results

Boys took more steps than the girls overall ($t = 3.86$, $p = .001$), at recess ($t = 4.16$, $p = .001$), and at lunch ($t = 2.50$, $p = .015$) regardless of uniform type (Table 1). The mean steps per minute were based on 15 minutes and 20 minutes of activity during recess and lunch respectively.

Table 2 provides the unadjusted mean step counts for males and females according to occasion and uniform type. The mixed model analyses found that girls, but not boys, were significantly more active at recess, lunch and overall when wearing their sports uniform compared to their winter uniform. The girls took more steps during recess (128) and lunch (176) when wearing their sports uniform than when wearing their winter uniform. The boys marginally increased their step counts during recess and overall but the differences were not significant. When the data for the total sample were considered and controlling for gender, mean step counts were significantly higher at recess and overall when the sports uniform was worn.

The participants recorded their perceived intensity of effort (1, 2 or

Table 1 Mean pedometer steps and steps per minute for combined, recess and lunch breaks for boys (n=36) and girls (n=24)

	Combined	Recess		Lunch	
	Mean	Mean	Steps/min	Mean	Steps/min
	M (SD)	M (SD)	M (SD)	M (SD)	M (SD)
Boys	1310.0 (347.6)	1134.1 (471.3)	75.6	1460.3 (378.5)	73.0
Girls	1031.8 (227.3)	735.0 (211.7)	49.0	1251.3 (259.7)	62.5

Note: All gender differences significant p B.01.

Table 2 Unadjusted mean daily pedometer steps for winter and sports uniforms during combined and separate incidental breaks

	Recess			Lunch			Total		
	Winter	Sports	p	Winter	Sports	p	Winter	Sports	p
	M (SD)	M (SD)		M (SD)	M (SD)		M (SD)	M (SD)	
Boys	1036.1 (345.1)	1127.1 (532.6)	0.16	1485.4 (374.7)	1455.8 (539.4)	0.82	1275.5 (331.9)	1364 (522.0)	0.37
Girls	690.1 (275.0)	818.2 (244.5)	0.03	1172.6 (296.5)	1348.3 (368.3)	0.04	933.3 (271.8)	1134.1 (271.9)	0.006
Total	884.7 (358.5)	1050.7 (441.5)	0.02	1348.5 (376.2)	1408.1 (470.7)	0.17	1125.8 (349.4)	1261.9 (441.5)	0.02

Note: p values based on linear mixed model analyses.

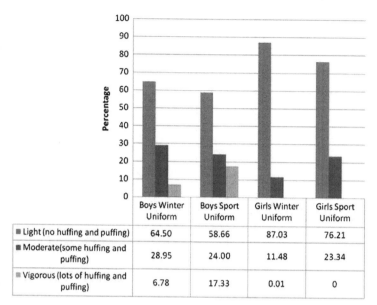

	Boys Winter Uniform	Boys Sport Uniform	Girls Winter Uniform	Girls Sport Uniform
▪ Light (no huffing and puffing)	64.50	58.66	87.03	76.21
▪ Moderate(some huffing and puffing)	28.95	24.00	11.48	23.34
▪ Vigorous (lots of huffing and puffing)	6.78	17.33	0.01	0

Figure 2 Prevalence (%) of perceived intensity of males and females for all breaks.

3) after each activity period. The number of occasions where each intensity level was reported were summed for boys and girls when wearing each uniform type (Figure 2).

More low-intensity play breaks were reported for both boys and girls during play breaks regardless of uniform type. Of interest, when sports uniform was worn, the prevalence of vigorous-intensity occasions increased for boys (6.8 % to 17.3%) and the prevalence of moderate-intensity occasions increased for the girls from 11.5 % to 23.3%). Girls only reported five play occasions (four wearing winter uniform and one wearing sport uniform) as vigorous. For each participant, the intensity scores were converted to a mean composite score for each uniform condition (see Table 3). There were no gender, uniform or occasion differences in perceived intensity (Table 3), although a trend was apparent for the girls. At both recess and lunch, girls had a higher mean perceived intensity when wearing sports uniform.

Table 3 Perceived intensity of activities M (SD) for recess and lunch according to uniform type

	Recess			Lunch			Total		
	Winter	Sports	p	Winter	Sports	p	Winter	Sports	p
	M (SD)	M (SD)		M (SD)	M (SD)		M (SD)	M (SD)	
Boys	1.42(.40)	1.49(.56)	.73	1.52(.46)	1.40(.50)	.22	1.44(.37)	1.46(.57)	.87
Girls	1.13(.34)	1.24(.32)	.22	1.15(.30)	1.27(.35)	.14	1.14(.31)	1.25(.30)	.17
Total	1.25(.39)	1.33(.45)	.24	1.30(.41)	1.33(.42)	.74	1.27(.37)	1.34(.44)	.28

Discussion

The primary purpose of the study was to examine the effect of school uniform on physical activity during school play breaks, and if the effect differed between girls and boys. The results revealed that girls, but not boys, took more steps during play breaks when wearing sports uniform compared to winter uniform. Although perceived intensity levels of the play breaks increased for both boys and girls when wearing sports uniform, it appears that this increase was more apparent in the girls than the boys. Light activity was the most prevalent intensity level for both boys and girls across both uniform types.

Regardless of uniform type, the boys took more steps during recess and lunch than girls which is consistent with many other school-based studies, (Beighle, Morgan, Masurier, & Pangrazi, 2006; Vincent & Pangrazi, 2002), however the mean steps per minutes for males and females were much lower at recess and lunch than those reported in other studies (Beighle & Pangrazi, 2006; Loucaides & Jago, 2008; Tudor-Locke et al., 2006). The researchers were unable to identify any specific data for 10-year-old children, however Beighle and Pangrazi (2006) suggested a mean of 90 steps per minute is typical of nine-year-old children. For primary-school-aged children, Tudor-Locke et al. (2006) reported means of 99.3 steps/min and 67.4 steps/ min and Loucaides and Jago (2008) reported 72.2 steps/ min and 51.9 steps/min for males and females respectively during recess. Given these ranging levels, further studies are needed to better determine mean steps per minute for boys and girls of different ages.

The gender difference in steps per minute could be attributed to differences in the intensity of play patterns. In this study, a higher prevalence of play breaks with a perceived vigorous intensity were reported by boys than girls. Others have reported that boys tend to dominate available playground space as they engage in more vigorous activities such as competitive games like soccer and football, chase games, or rough-and-tumble play requiring speed, strength, endurance, and aggression (Beighle et al., 2008; Pellegrini, Blatchford, Kato, & Baines, 2004). On the other hand, girls participate in more sedentary activities (Ridgers, Stratton, & Fairclough, 2006).

Uniform type had a greater impact on physical activity level among the girls than the boys. They were significantly more active at both recess and lunch when wearing their sports uniform compared to their winter uniform. Other studies have found that changing the structural environment can impact on physical activity, especially in relation to girls. Verstraete et al. (2006) found providing game equipment at recess was effective in girls, but not in boys. Similar to the current study, Verstraete et al. (2006) indicated that the boys had high physical-activity levels prior to the game equipment being introduced, making it difficult to find significant improvements. In this study, boys had similar step counts in both conditions and boys were significantly more active than girls in both uniform conditions over the four weeks. Therefore, the boys already had higher physical activity levels in the winter uniform condition, and, similar to the study by Verstraete et al. (2006) it was difficult to find significant improvements when they were in the sport uniform condition. Conversely, as the girls had lower physical-activity levels than boys in the winter uniform condition, they had the opportunity to show a significant difference when wearing the sport uniform. It appears that the winter uniform for boys does not adversely impact on their ability to be physically active whereas the restrictive nature of the winter uniform for girls has the opposite effect. It should be noted that the winter uniform for boys requires long trousers whereas a skirt is required for girls. It is not such a big change in uniform when moving from trousers to a sport tracksuit however; moving from a skirt to sports tracksuit is clearly a greater change for the girls.

This study also questioned if intensity would change if the type of uniform changed. Although minimal, students engaged in slightly more vigorous activities when wearing their sports uniform and this did not differ significantly between boys and girls. Ridgers et al. (2007) indicated that while boys are more active overall during play time, boys and girls experienced comparable increases in their recess Moderate to Vigorous Physical Activity (MVPA) and Vigorous Physical Activity (VPA) following the playground markings and physical structures intervention. Perhaps the reason this study did not capture any major changes in intensity was the nature of the measurement. There were only three choices to rate intensity level, making it difficult to detect any significant change. Students also may not have clearly understood how each statement and face was related to each feeling after being physically active. Although they recorded responses in the log book immediately after the play break there was no way to determine if the intensity of the activity varied in the break. For example they may have engaged in vigorous activity for the first 10 minutes, but not in the last 5 minutes of the break. Therefore, recording how they felt immediately after the break may not actually reflect the intensity of their activities over the entire break.

In addition, although the three intensity categories were explained to the students prior to the study, some students may have overestimated or underestimated their intensity.

Strengths and Limitations

This is the first study to identify a negative effect of school uniform on activity levels in primary school children; however as the small pilot study involved a convenience sample from one year group in one school the study needs to be replicated with a larger sample. Some events may have prevented the students from engaging in physical activity during the play breaks and it was not possible to record all of these. As discussed above, the scale used for the students to report perceived intensity may not have been sufficiently discriminatory to detect change, or sufficiently detailed to monitor variations in intensity over the play break.

In conclusion, the increase in mean steps, especially in females, and the slight increase in intensity when wearing the sports uniform reported in this study are important given that many children do not meet the recommended daily physical activity level of 60 minutes (Department of Health and Aging, 2004). Any strategies that increase the potential to be physically active should not be ignored. Schools are able to provide opportunities for young people to be physically active (Al-Nakeeb, Duncan, Lyons, & Woodfield, 2007; Booth, 1997; Tudor-Locke et al., 2006) and a range of school-based interventions have lead to increases in children's physical activity (Alfonso & Botelho, 2003; Ridgers, Stratton, Fairclough, & Twisk, 2006; Scruggs et al.,

2003; Stratton, 2000; Stratton & Leonnard, 2002; Stratton & Mullan, 2003; Sutterby & Frost, 2002; Verstraete et al., 2006; Zask et al., 2001). School policies may either enhance this potential or create barriers (Marron, 2008). Clearly structural changes to the school environment can be successful in encouraging physical activity levels. In the case of this study, it was a simple change in the type of uniform worn.

Notes on Contributors

Hannah Norrish completed her Bachelor in Health and Physical Education (honours) in 2010. She was awarded first class honours and the findings from her research project, The Effect of School Uniform on Incidental Physical Activity among 10-year-old children, provided the basis of this article. Hannah is now teaching in a country primary school in Western Australia.

Fiona Farringdon is Assistant Dean, Health Sciences and coordinates the Bachelor of Preventive Health. She has been involved in health education and health promotion for over twenty five years at the practitioner and academic levels and previously taught at a variety of secondary and primary schools as a health and physical education teacher for ten years. Her research interests include the efficacy of school-based health education programmes; reducing alcohol and other drug related harm for individuals and communities, eating patterns of adolescents, increasing physical activity levels in children and adolescents and mental health in adolescents.

Max Bulsara holds the chair in Biostatistics at the University of Notre Dame in Western Australia. He has been involved in epidemiological studies for over two decades both overseas and in Australia, and a number of research projects relating to the physical activity, built environment and health.

Beth Hands has been involved in research involving children and adolescents for two decades. She is currently the Director of the Institute for Health and Rehabilitation Research at the University of Notre Dame. She authored the highly regarded Fundamental Movement Skills Teacher Resource and Play5 Teacher Manual.

References

Afonso, B., & Botelho, G. (2003). Promoting informal physical activity at school recess: A pilot study with girls and boys from 2nd and 4th grades of elementary school. *Revista Portuguesa de Ciencias do Desporto, 3*(2), 143–145.

Al-Nakeeb, Y., Duncan, M. J., Lyons, M., & Woodfield, L. (2007). Body fatness and physical activity levels of young children. *Annals of Human Biology, 34*(1), 1–12.

Barfield, J. P., Rowe, D., & Michael, T. (2004). Interinstrument reliability of the Yamax Digiwalker in elementary school children. *Measurement in Physical Education & Exercise Science, 8*, 109–116.

Bassett, D. R., Ainsworth, B. E., Swartz, A. M., Stratch, S. J., O'Brien, W. L., & King, G. A. (2000). Validity of four motion sensors in measuring moderate intensity physical activity. *Medicine and Science in Sports and Exercise, 32*, s5417–s5418.

Beighle, A., Alderman, B., Morgan, C.F., & Le Masurier, G. (2008). Seasonality in children's pedometer-measured physical activity levels. *Research Quarterly for Exercise and Sport, 79*(2), 256–261.

Beighle, A., Morgan, C. F., Le Masurier, G., & Pangrazi, R. P. (2006). Children's physical activity during recess and outside of school. *Journal of School Health, 76*(10), 516–520.

Beighle, A., & Pangrazi, R. P. (2006). Measuring children's activity levels: The association between step counts and activity time. *Journal of Physical Activity and Health, 3*, 221–229.

Biddle, S., Coalter, F., O'Donovan, T., MacBeth, J., Nevill, M., & Whitehead, S. (2005). *Increasing demand for sport and physical activity by girls.* Edinburgh: SportScotland.

Booth, M. (1997). The 1997 NSW schools fitness and physical activity survey. *NSW Public Health Bulletin, 8*(5), 35–36.

Coakley, J., & White, A. (1992). Making decisions: Gender and sport participation among British adolescents. *Social Sport Journal, 9*(1), 20–35.

Connolly, P., & McKenzie, T. L. Effects of a games intervention on the physical activity levels of children at recess. *Research Quarterly for Exercise and Sport, 66*(1), A60.

Cratty, B. J., Ikeda, N., Martin, M. M. M., Jennett, C., & Morris, M. (1970). *Game choices of children with movement problems.* Springfield, IL: CC Thomas.

Department of Education. (2012). School uniforms. Retrieved February 29, 2012, from http://det.wa.edu.au/schoolsandyou/detcms/navigation/parents-and-community/life-at-school/?oid=Category-id-3869966#toc2.

Department of Health and Aging. (2004). *Australia's physical activity recommendations for 5-12 year olds.* Canberra: Commonwealth of Australia.

Gretebeck, R. J., & Montoye, H. J. (1992). Variability of some objective measures of physical activity. *Medicine and Science in Sports and Exercise, 24*(10), 1167–1172.

Hands, B., Parker, H., Glasson, C., Brinkman, S., & Read, H. (2004). *Physical activity and nutrition levels in Western Australian children and adolescents: Physical activity report.* Perth: Government of Western Australia.

Hands, B., Parker, H., & Larkin, D. (2006). Physical activity measurement methods for young children: A comparative study. *Measurement in Physical Education and Exercise Science, 10*(3), 203–214.

Harper, L., & Sanders, K. (1975). Preschool children's use of space: Sex differences in outdoor play. *Developmental Psychology, 11*, 119.

Kohl, H. W., & Hobbs, K. E. (1998). Development of physical activity behaviors among children and adolescents. *Pediatrics, 101*(3), 549–554.

Loucaides, C. A., Chedzoy, S. M., & Bennett, N. (2003). Pedometer-assessed physical (ambulatory) activity in Cypriot children. *European Physical Education Review, 9*(1), 43–55.

Loucaides, C. A., & Jago, R. (2008). Differences in physical activity by gender, weight status, and travel mode to school in Cypriot children. *Preventive Medicine, 47*(1), 107–111.

Marron, S. (2008). *An analysis of break time active play in Irish primary schools* (Unpublished master's thesis). Waterford Institute of Technology, Waterford, Ireland

McKenzie, T. L., Sallis, J. F., Elder, J. P., Berry, C. C., Hoy, P. L., Nader, P., Zive, M., & Broyles, S. (1997). Physical activity levels and prompts in young children at recess: A two-year study of a bi-ethnic sample. *Research Quarterly for Exercise and Sport, 68*(3), 195–202.

Morgan, F., Graser, S. V., & Pangrazi, R. P. (2008). A prospective study of pedometer-determined physical activity and physical self-perceptions in children. *Research Quarterly for Exercise and Sport, 79*(2), 133–141.

Orme, J. (1991). Adolescent girls and exercise: too much of a struggle? *Education and Health, 9*, 76–80.

Pate, R. R., Baranowski, T., Dowda, M., & Trost, S. (1996). Tracking of physical activity in young children. *Medicine and Science in Sports and Exercise, 28*, 92–96.

Pellegrini, A. D., Blatchford, P., Kato, K., & Baines, E. (2004). A short-term longitudinal study of children's playground games in primary school: Implications for adjustment to school and social adjustment in the USA and the UK. *Social Development, 13*(1), 107–123.

Pfister, G. (1993). Appropriation of the environment, motor experiences and sporting activities of girls and women. International *Review for Sociology of Sport, 28*, 159–171.

Porter, S. (2002). *Physical activity: An exploration of the issues and attitudes of teenage girls.* London, UK: Scott Porter Research and Marketing.

Reilly, T., & Stratton, G. (1995). Children and adolescents in sport: Physiological considerations. *Sports Exercise and Injury, 1,* 207–213.

Ridgers, N. D., Stratton, G., & Fairclough, J. (2006). Physical activity levels of children during school playtime. *Sports Medicine, 36*(4), 359–371.

Ridgers, N. D., Stratton, G., Fairclough, J., & Twisk, J. W. R. (2006). Long term effects of playground markings and physical structures on children's recess physical activity levels. *Preventive Medicine, 44*(5), 393–397.

Ridgers, N. D., Stratton, G., Fairclough, S., & Twisk, J. (2007). Children's physical activity levels during school recess: A quasi-experimental intervention study. International *Journal of the American Medicine Association, 282*(16), 1561–1567.

Rowlands, A. V., & Hughes, D. R. (2006). Variability of physical activity patterns by type of day and season in 8-10 year old boys. *Research Quarterly for Exercise and Sport, 77*(1), 391–395.

Sallis, J. F. (1991). Self-report measures of children's physical activity. *Journal of School Health, 61*(5), 215-224.

Sallis, J. F., Conway, T. L., Prochaska, J. J., McKenzie, T. L., Marshall, S. J., & Brown, M. (2001). The association of school environments with youth physical activity. *American Journal of Public Health, 91*(4), 618-620.

Sallis, J. F., Prochaska, J. J., & Taylor, W. C. (2000). A review of correlates of physical activity of children and adolescents. *Medicine and Science in Sports and Exercise, 32*(5), 963-975.

Scruggs, P. W., Beveridge, S. K., & Watson, D. L. (2003). Increasing children's school time physical activity using structured fitness breaks. *Pediatric Exercise Science, 15*(2), 156–169.

Sidman, C. L., Vincent, S. D., Corbin, C. B., Pangrazi, R. P., & Vincent, W. J. (2001). Digital pedometers: Checking calibration prior to use in research. *Medicine and Science in Sports and Exercise, 33*(5), 299.

Singer, J., & Willett, J. (2003). *Applied longitudinal data analysis: Modeling change and event occurrence.* New York: Oxford University Press.

Sirard, J. R., & Pate, R. R. (2001). Physical activity assessment in children and adolescents. *Sports Medicine, 31*(6), 439–454.

Stanley, R. M., Ridley, K., & Olds, T. S. (2011). The type and prevalence of activities performed by Australian children during the lunchtime and after school periods. *Journal of Science and Medicine in Sport, 14,* 227–232.

Stratton, G. (2000). Promoting children's physical activity in primary school: An intervention study using playground markings. *Ergonomics, 43*(10), 1538–1546.

Stratton, G., & Leonard, J. (2002). The metabolism of the elementary school playground: The effects of an intervention study on children's energy expenditure. *Pediatric Exercise Science, 14*(2), 170–180.

Stratton, G., & Mota, J. (2000). Girls' physical activity during primary school playtime: A validation study using systematic observation and heart rate telemetry. *Journal of Human Movement Studies, 33*, 18–26.

Stratton, G., & Mullan, E. (2003). The effect of playground markings on children's physical activity levels. *Revista Portuguesa Ciê^n-cias do Desporto, 3*(1), S137.

Sutterby, J. A., & Frost, J. L. (2002). Making playgrounds fit for children and children fit on playgrounds. *Young Children, 57*(3), 36–42.

Trost, S., Pate, R. R., Freedson, P. S., Sallis, J. F., & Taylor, W. C. (2000). Using objective physical activity measures with youth: How many days of monitoring are needed? *Medicine and Science in Sports and Exercise, 32*(2), 426–431.

Tudor-Locke, C., Lee, S. M., Morgan, C. F., Beighle, A., & Pangrazi, R. P. (2006). Children's pedometer-determined physical activity during the segmented school day. *Medicine and Science in Sports and Exercise, 38*(10), 1732–1738.

Tudor-Locke, C., Williams, J. E., Reis, J. P., & Pluto, D. (2002). Utility of pedometers for assessing physical activity: Convergent validity. *Sports Medicine, 32*(12), 795–808.

Verstraete, S., Cardon, G., DeClercq, D., & Bourdeaudhuij, I. D. (2006). Increasing children's physical activity levels during recess periods in elementary schools: The effects of providing game equipment. *European Journal of Public Health, 16*(4), 415–419.

Vincent, S. D., & Pangrazi, R. P. (2002). Determining baseline physical activity levels in children. *Pediatric Exercise Science, 14*, 432–441.

World Health Organisation. (2008). Physical activity and young people. Retrieved October 11, 2008, from http://www.who.int/dietphysicalactivity/factsheet_young_people/en.

Zask, A., Beurden, E., Barnett, L., Brooks, L. O., & Dietrich, U. C. (2001). Active school playgrounds: Myth or reality? Results of the 'Move it Groove it' project. *Preventive Medicine, 33*(1), 401–408.

Index